The Church

The Church

by

Johann Andreas Quenstedt

Theologia Didactico-Polemica
Part IV, Chapter XV: *De ecclesia*
Third edition, 1696

edited, abridged, translated, and briefly
annotated
by
Luther Poellot

REPRISTINATION PRESS
MALONE, TEXAS

Copyright 1999 by Luther Poellot. Published by permission of the translator. No part of this publication may be reproduced, stored in a retrieval system, or transmitted, in any form or by any means, electronic, mechanical, photocopying or otherwise without the prior written permission of Repristination Press.

Hardcover edition published 1999;
paperback edition published in 2019

REPRISTINATION PRESS
716 HCR 3424 E
MALONE, TEXAS 76660

E-mail: HUNNIUS@AOL.COM

ISBN 9781891469381

Table of Contents

Translator's Preface	vii
Abbreviations	ix
Section I: Didactic—35 Theses	1
Section II: Polemic	

Question I
    Is the church properly and principally
    the assembly of saints and true believers?   35

Question II
    Is the church rightly distinguished into visible
    and invisible?   53

Question III
    I. Can the whole catholic and invisible church
    (or one and all of the believers and the elect)
    together and at once err and go astray in the
    fundamental articles of faith, indeed not
    finally but temporarily?
    II. [Can] the visible church sometimes so err in
        faith and morals that it goes completely
    astray?   67

Question IV
    Are the essential and perpetual marks of the
    church the pure preaching of the divine Word
    and the proper use of the Sacraments?   87

Question V
    Is the Roman pontiff the absolute ruler and head
    of the catholic church?   107

Question VI
    Is the power to convoke councils and preside over
    them in the hands of the emperor, or princes, or
    rather in the hands of the Roman pontiff?   129

> *Do not despise the writings of the old faithful church fathers, the writings of a Luther, Chemnitz, Quenstedt, Gerhard, H. Müller, etc. Otherwise you disobey the Holy Spirit, who commands you: "Do not despise prophecy" [that is, exposition of Scripture; 1 The. 5:20].*
>
>   C. F. W. Walther
>   1884 Synodical Conference convention essay

Translator's Preface

Luther says: "We correctly confess in our holy Christian Creed that we *believe* a holy church. For it is invisible, dwells in the spirit at a place into which no one can penetrate; therefore its holiness cannot be seen" (translated from the St. Louis ed., IX, 702). A patient and unbiased searcher may find some roots of the distinction between the visible and the invisible church in Augustine, *Breviculus collationis cum Donatistis*. See also Luke 17:20–21 and 1 Kin. 19:13–18. So much for those who do not grasp and/or do not like the distinction and dismiss it as little more than the product of post-Reformation wordsmiths.

Other parts of this chapter of Quenstedt's *Theologia* pertinent to our time include those on the marks of the church and on the claim of a "vicar of Christ" to be head of the visible church.

Some have expressed interest in having the (very long) chapter on Holy Scripture or perhaps even all 48 chapters of the *Theologia* in English. Five have now appeared (three as *The Nature and Character of Theology*, Concordia Publishing House, St. Louis, Mo., 1986; one as *The Holy Ministry*, Concordia Theological Seminary, Fort Wayne, Ind., 1991). The present translator began his work without publication in mind on March 15, 1979, and wrote at the top of the first page: "This venture I shall not finish." He hopes that all critics of his work will be gentle and that perhaps some of them will in turn improve upon it and possibly nurse it along farther to completion.

As for the art of translation: in this case its demands span not only languages as such and the cultures they served but also centuries of time. Its challenges are at times daunting, and the final product may leave something to be desired. The word *papist* (for the Latin *pontificius*) is not always and not necessarily disparaging (as it may be at times or in the minds of some readers); it serves also (as it has since at least 1582) simply to identify a Roman Catholic who is a partisan of the pope. Let the context speak to the subject—and let the author speak for himself.

    The author, Quenstedt (1617–88), professor at the university of Wittenberg, Germany, was the foremost leader of orthodox Lutheranism. His Theologia, first published 1681, was reissued 1691, 1696, 1701, 1702, and 1715. The relationship between church and state is different in our day from what it was in his, as is clear especially from Theses XXVI and XXVIII and Question VI.

Abbreviations

Genesis	Gen.	Zechariah	Zec.
Exodus	Exo.	Malachi	Mal.
Leviticus	Lev.		
Numbers	Num.	Matthew	Mat.
Deuteronomy	Deu.	Romans	Rom.
Joshua	Jos.	1 Corinthians	1 Cor.
Judges	Jud.	2 Corinthians	2 Cor.
1 Samuel	1 Sam.	Galatians	Gal.
2 Samuel	2 Sam.	Ephesians	Eph.
1 Kings	1 Kin.	Philippians	Phi.
2 Kings	2 Kin.	Colossians	Col.
1 Chronicles	1 Chr.	1 Thessalonians	1 The.
2 Chronicles	2 Chr.	2 Thessalonians	2 The.
Nehemiah	Neh.	1 Timothy	1 Tim.
Esther	Est.	2 Timothy	2 Tim.
Psalms	Psa.	Titus	Tit.
Proverbs	Pro.	Philemon	Phm.
Song of Solomon	SSo.	Hebrews	Heb.
Isaiah	Isa.	James	Jam.
Jeremiah	Jer.	1 Peter	1 Ptr.
Lamentations	Lam.	2 Peter	2 Ptr.
Ezekiel	Eze.	Revelation	Rev.
Daniel	Dan.		
Hosea	Hos.		
Obadiah	Oba.		
Jonah	Jon.		
Micah	Mic.		
Nahum	Nah.		
Habakkuk	Hab.		
Zephaniah	Zep.		
Haggai	Hag.		

Section I: Didactic

Thesis I

The whole group[1] that the three hierarchical estates—ecclesiastical, political, and economical—form is called *ecclesia*.

Thesis II

The word *ecclesia* is Greek in origin, deriving ἀπὸ τοῦ ἐκκαλεῖν, from "to call out"; so that ἐκκλησία is, by the thrust of the word, a "calling out,"[2] brought about by the voice[3] of the one who issues the call,[4] or the assembly[5] of those who are called out of another, larger community.

Note: By reason of the particle ἐκ, the word ἐκκλησία denotes (1) separation, with regard to the starting point[6] [and] (2) the gathering, or congregation, with respect to the end point,[7] as it may so be called because, called out of mankind, it is gathered into a holy assembly.[8] The word ecclesia is never used for any one person. For a congregation and gathering is only of more. An ecclesia is therefore any whole body or assembly consisting not in any one individual arrogating title, office, and privileges to himself, but is composed on the whole of all the faithful in this world or at least of some teachers and hearers as like-minded and integrating members.

Thesis III

The word *ecclesia* is used either [1] broadly and in general for any assembly and gathering, either sacred or secular, Acts 19:32, 39, or [2] in a narrow and particular sense; and, of course, in a bad or in a good sense.

Note: The word *ecclesia* in a wide sense and in general is used also for political and secular gatherings, as in Eze. 32:3, ἐκκλησίᾳ λαῶν πολλῶν [in a company of many people] and Acts 19:32, "the assembly was in confusion," ἐκκλησία συγκεχυμένη. In v. 29 it denotes the gathering of citizens who streamed together into the theater. In vv. 39–49 it is called ἔννομος ἐκκλησία, a lawful assembly, namely held on a certain day or a legal gathering of judges and parties. In Psa. 26:5 it is used in a narrow and particular sense and, what is more, for the assembly of the wicked; here the Septuagint translates: "ἐμίσησα ἐκκλησίαν πονηρεθομένων [I have hated the assembly of evildoers]"; Vulgate: "I hate the assembly of evildoers," which is the "synagogue of Satan," Rev. 2:9; 3:9. But taken in a good sense it designates a holy assembly, or [the congregation] of believers, Mat. 16:18; Acts 20:28; 1 Cor. 1:2; 10:32; etc. And in order that this holy assembly might be distinguished from secular gatherings, it is called the *ecclesia* [church] of God, Acts 20:28; 1 Cor. 1:2; Gal. 1:13, and *ecclesia* [church] of the saints, 1 Cor. 14:33.

Thesis IV

And taken thus in a good sense it denotes either the synthetic church,[9] e.g., Mat. 16:18; 1 Tim. 3:15, or the representative [church].

Note: We call that [church] synthetic which consists of the whole universal world of believers, both teachers and hearers, of the present, past, and future time and designates the inward and outward fellowship of believers in the one church. Teachers and some leaders of churches are called the representative church, since they can present and explain the public doctrine of the church more fully and better than hearers alone apart from teachers. And the representative church is either the universal or the particular church, [consisting] of one or more, which is resolved by number into many teachers and more-eminent laymen.[10]

The Synthetic Church

Thesis V

[The term] "synthetic church" is used [I] in a wide sense and γενικῶς [in a general way] for the common assembly of all the called who use the preaching of the Word and the Sacraments, [and II] in a narrow sense and in particular for the assembly of saints, or of believers, included in that general assembly.

Note: Though, taken in a wide sense, the word ecclesia denotes an outward, visible fellowship that is held together by the bond of profession of the same true doctrine and of partaking of the Sacraments—in which fellowship many are wicked and hypocrites (regarding whom [cf.] Art. VIII of the Augsburg Confession), who indeed are in the church but not of the church, that is, they are not living members of the church, though they adhere to it, for they adhere only as dead and putrid members, just as the withered hand [clung to] Jeroboam [1 Kin. 13:4]—yet used in a narrow sense and properly, the word *ecclesia* denotes the assembly of saints, or of believers. I say with the Augsburg Confession, Art. VII, "of saints," not of the elect, (1) lest any turn the word *elect* to the Calvinistic meaning regarding the elect by absolute decree of God and (2) because the terms *saints* and *believers* are wider than elect. For not only the elect belong to the church, but also the πρόσκαιροι [temporary] believers, or those who believe for a while, as Christ says, Luke 8:13.

Thesis VI

The church of the saints is either triumphant in heaven, Heb. 12:22-23, or militant on earth, under the banner of the cross.

Note: The church of the saints is [1] either triumphant in heaven; translated to heavenly rest from the labor of fighting and set free from the danger of being overcome, it triumphs in heaven over all enemies, Heb. 12:22-23: "You have come to Mount Zion and [to] the city of the living God, the heavenly Jerusalem, and to the church of the firstborn, who are enrolled in heaven." These words describe the church militant on earth and the church triumphant in heaven as one assembly and one congregation. But how have the Hebrews come to Mount Zion? Because by the preaching of the Gospel, begun in Jerusalem, they were called and gathered to the fellowship of the church of the New Testament, Luke 24:47, which was also prefigured by Mount Zion and the city of Jerusalem and often designated in the Old Testament by that name. But we are not to make meticulous distinctions here as to which things, then, belong to the church militant and which to the church triumphant in this statement, or to believe that they are presented in sequence, for it is seen, as I have said, as one body and one assembly. [2] Or it is militant on earth, namely that assembly which under the banner of Christ contends constantly against the devil, the world, and the flesh.

Thesis VII

The church militant is either universal, Mat. 16:18; Eph. 1:22; 5:24-27; [and] 1 Tim. 3:15, or particular.

Note: The church militant is either universal (as it were worldwide[11]) or particular. Mat. 16:18 speaks of the *universal* church: "You are Peter, and on this rock I will build My church." Observe: By "rock" is meant [1] either Peter's faith in Christ [2] or [his] ἐξομολόγησις, that is, the confession of faith in Christ that Peter made ("You are the Christ, the Son of the living God," as Chrysostom and Theophylact [have it] on this passage). [3] Or Christ Himself, namely He whom Peter confessed, as Augustine in many passages teaches accurately and extensively, and with him very many [other] fathers, that the word "rock" is to be taken in this passage. Paul [puts it] best of all, 1 Cor. 3:11: "Other foundation can no one lay than that which is laid, which is Christ Jesus"; Eph. 1:22, where Christ is called the Head of the church, namely the universal [church]; cf. Eph. 5:23–27; Col. 1:18, where He is called "ἡ κεφαλὴ τοῦ σώματος τῆς ἐκκλησίας, the Head of the body, the church,"; [and] 1 Tim. 3:15, where the church is called "the pillar and foundation of the truth." In these passages, I say, the word "church" is used in the universal sense, for the whole assembly of true believers, as it were, of the elect. The *particular* church is any particular assembly under the one Head, Christ, gathered by Word and Sacrament in a certain place, and it is either diocesan in a certain realm and dominion, or provincial in a certain city and village, or domestic in a certain family. And a single family is called church three times in the New Testament: Rom. 16:5; Col. 4:15; and Phm. 2.

Thesis VIII

The church universal is such either absolutely or relatively. The universal church in the absolute sense is the assembly consisting of the believers of all places and times, whom God has called by the preaching of the Word to the communion of the actual, spiritual, and heavenly blessings ever since the beginning of the world and still today calls and will call to the end of the world. The church [that is] relatively universal is the assembly of all believers who continue steadfastly at the same time anywhere in the world in one and the same fellowship of faith, grace, salvation, and love.

Note 1: The church is called universal for a twofold reason: (1) by reason of place; (2) by reason of time. By reason of place, that assembly is called the universal church, which is called together by Word and Sacraments out of various peoples throughout the whole world to the fellowship of the church and participation of the blessings of Christ. And by reason of time, that assembly [is called the universal church], which is gathered by the Word at different times from the beginning of the world to its end. And so the church universal in the absolute sense, by reason of place as well as by reason of time, is the assembly of true believers that God has called from the beginning of the world to its consummation from all peoples and nations, through the preaching of the Word, to the communion of actual, spiritual, and heavenly blessings, and still today calls and will call and gather to the end of the world.

Note 2: The church that is universal in a relative sense is the assembly of all true believers who at the same time, for example, of the Old or of the New Testament or also today, anywhere in the world, continue steadfastly in one and the same inner fellowship of faith, grace, love, and salvation. Here observe: (1) The universality of time includes the universality of place, but not the other way around. (2) The discussion is not about just any fellowship, but about the inner [fellowship] of faith, grace, and salvation, in which only true believers and the elect participate.

Thesis IX

The particular church is the assembly not of all but of some believers in a certain place, of those who are called to participate in salvation and who continue steadfastly in inner spiritual fellowship.

Note: The church is called particular also in a twofold way: (1) by reason of time [and] (2) by reason of place. By reason of time, the church of the Old Testament [is] one [and] that of the New Testament [is] another. By reason of place, one is gathered by God in some whole realm, another in some city, or also [in] a house. Hence the apostles speak not only of the church κατ'οἶκον [in a house], Rom. 16:5, and τῇ ἐν Κορίνθῳ [that (is) in Corinth], 1 Cor. 1:2, but in the plural, of churches τῶν ἐθνῶν [of the Gentiles], Rom. 16:4, τὰς τῆς Γαλατίας καὶ τῆς Ἰοθδαίας [those in Galatia and in Judaea], Gal. 1:2, 22, [and] τὰς ἐν τῇ Ἀσίᾳ [those in Asia], Rev. 1:4.

Thesis X

Used in a wider sense, [the term] "synthetic church" denotes the outward mixed assembly of the called, such an assembly [being] either public, consisting of pastors and hearers of all ranks, Rev. 1:4, or private, as also families enjoy the name "church," Col. 4:15.

Note: Though an outward mixed assembly of the called never lacks elect and true believers, yet it is a mixture of good and wicked, of the elect and the reprobate, or hypocrites. And this assembly, insofar as it strikes the eyes through outward profession, is either [1] public, consisting of pastors and hearers of all ranks; the word *church* is thus used Rev. 1:4: "John, to the seven churches that [are] in Asia" etc., or [2] private, as also Christian families enjoy the name "church," Rom. 16:5: "Greet the church that is in their (Aquila's and Priscilla's) house," [and] Col. 4:15: "Greet Nymphas and the church that is in his house"; cf. Phm. 2.

Thesis XI

Taken improperly, the word *church* is used either metonymically for a public place in which it gathers for religious worship, or synecdochically for a part of the church; and it is thus [synecdochically] used either for the presbytery, Mat. 18:17, or for the hearers only, who elsewhere are known by the name "flock," Acts 20:28; 1 Ptr. 5:2.

Note 1: The metonymical meaning of the word *church*—namely for a building in which people usually assemble to observe sacred rites, or for a place of assembly—does not occur indisputably in the Holy Scriptures. König indeed cites the passage in 1 Cor. 11:18: "When you come together in the church," where Grotius notes: "That is, in the house in which the meetings are held." Others add also the passage in [1 Cor.] 14:34: "Let the women be silent in the churches." But the matter itself shows that not a church building but the very gathering of Christian people, or the assembly of the church, is meant by the name in both cases. John Cameron maintains against the papists that in the New Testament the word *church* never means a place. And as to what Bellarmine stresses, that to come together in church is not to gather in an assembly but in a place, he replies: "Though one does not usually speak of coming together in an assembly, yet we speak of coming together in the senate, or synod," etc. And though in [1 Cor. 11:]22 "church" is used in contrast to private houses: "Have you not houses, or do you despise the church of God?" (on the basis of this, Bellarmine almost exults, but before victory), yet nothing can be definitely proved from this. For "church" can be set over against private houses, even though by this is not meant a place or a church building, but a church meeting. That the latter is meant is shown by what follows, in which those things explain each other: "Or do you despise the church of God and humiliate those who have nothing," that is, the poor? That church, namely, is despised to which the poor belong. And in the canon law, where consecration of a church, building and repairing of churches, etc. is discussed, it is also clear that the word *church* is used for a sacred building in which some particular church gathers to hear the Word and [for] divine worship.

Note 2: The word *church* is also used synecdochically for a part of it [the church], namely when the assembly of the church is divided into flock and shepherds; that is why the name "church," by the figure of synecdoche, is attached (1) to the presbytery, or church council, as in Mat. 18:17: "If he will not heed them, tell [it] to the church." The question here is whether the word *church* means—and that by the intent and meaning of Christ—the collective church [consisting] of sheep and shepherds, or only the representative church [consisting] of shepherds. I say, on the basis of the meaning and purpose of Christ, that more are meant than two or three; this is clear from the series of steps, which rises from fewer to more: "Rebuke him between yourself and him alone; then take one or two along etc.; and if he will not heed these, tell [it] to the church; and if he will not heed the church, let him be to you as a heathen and a publican." Hence also all interpreters, both Greek and Latin, who lived in the first six centuries after the birth of Christ, explained the word *church* in this passage of the representative assembly and its particular [part] or also, according to the nature of the cases, of the representative assembly of the universal Christian church. No one understood it of a single individual (as the papists [understand it] today of the Roman pope), [as] representative of the church. And Bellarmine himself could not deny this. But from the verse that follows, one can gather that presbyters and leaders are here understood by "church." (2) To the hearers, who elsewhere are known by the name "flock," as in Acts 20:28 [and] 1 Ptr. 5:2; in these passages, bishops and presbyters are enjoined to feed the church. It is therefore clear that never and nowhere does the name "church" denote some one individual, since it is a collective name. And a collection is nothing if not of more [than one].

Thesis XII

Here the word *church* is used in a wider sense and properly, for a holy assembly, not only of believers, but of all kinds of the called, and therefore mixed, consisting of believers and wicked [people], or hypocrites—an outward and public [entity].

Thesis XIII

The efficient principal cause of the synthetic church is the Holy Trinity, the Father, Eph. 1:3-4; the Son, Acts 20:28 [and] Mat. 16:18; and the Holy Spirit, John 3:5; 1 Ptr. 1:12; John 14:16-17.

Note: Since the gathering of the church is an outward work, therefore it belongs to all the three persons of the Deity, yet with the order and distinction of the persons preserved, with regard to distinct manner of working: The Father brings the church as bride to His Son and prepares a wedding banquet for Him, Mat. 22:2; the Son is the bridegroom to whom the church is betrothed, 2 Cor. 11:2—in fact, He is the one who Himself bought her for Himself with His own blood, Acts 20:28. Hence He also did not hesitate to call her His church, Mat. 16:18. Through the ministry of the Word and the Sacraments the Holy Spirit cleanses and adorns the church as a bride for her husband, Eph. 5:27 [and] Rev. 21:2, and is the pledge that the heavenly bridegroom gives to the church as to His bride, Eph. 1:14; cf. John 3:5 [and] 1 Ptr. 1:12, and who abides with her forever, John 14:16-17.

Thesis XIV

The impulsive cause that moves God to gather the church for Himself out of mankind is either outward or inward. The outward [cause] is both the extreme misery of people and the merit of Christ, 2 Tim. 1:9: "He has called us with a holy calling, not according to our works," etc. [and] 1 Cor. 1:4: "For the grace of God that is given you in Christ Jesus" etc.; cf. 1 Tim. 2:6. The impulsive inward cause is the immense goodness, fatherly compassion, and free favor of God, ruling in the whole matter of our salvation, 2 Tim. 1:9.

Thesis XV

The ministerial cause that God uses in gathering and preserving the church are the ministers of the Word, Mat. 22:3; Luke 14:17; Eph. 4:11–12; 1 Cor. 3:9–10; 2 Cor. 5:20.

Note: The ministers of the Word are called hereto by God, so that, by preaching the divine Word and administering the Sacraments, they might gather and preserve the church. They are the servants whom the king, He who prepared the wedding banquet for His Son, sends to call those who are invited to the wedding banquet, Mat. 22:3—the servants whom that man, who prepared a great banquet, sends at the hour of supper, to say to those who were invited that they should come, Luke 14:17, that is, the pastors and teachers whom Christ, exalted to the right hand of God, gave for the full equipment of the saints, for the work of the ministry, for the upbuilding of the body of Christ, Eph. 4:11–12, σθνεργοὶ ἐν τῇ οἰκοδομῇ τοῦ θεοῦ [workers together in God's (work of) building], 1 Cor. 3:9, who are ambassadors for Christ, 2 Cor. 5:20.

Thesis XVI

The instrumental, or organic, cause is the Word and the Sacraments, Mat. 28:19–20; Eph. 2:20–21.

Note: The church on earth is gathered by God through the Word and the Sacraments, with the Holy Spirit working efficaciously, Mat. 28:19: "As you go, teach and baptize"; cf. Eph. 2:20-21. Miracles were also used of old in the church to be planted, but now they cease in the church that has been planted among Christians by ordinance of Christ, 1 Cor. 13:8; 14:22.

Thesis XVII

The material of which the synthetic church consists, as it is here considered by us, are all who are called, without distinction, saints as well as hypocrites, Mat. 10:16; 13:24-25, 47.

Note: Truly, many who are not saints [but] hypocrites and wicked are intermingled with the pious. For two kinds of people are gathered in the church: (1) those who are inwardly regenerated and renewed by the Holy Spirit, given true faith, [and] implanted in Christ and so become true and living members of the church. But some, lacking inward regeneration and holiness, join themselves to this association only by outward fellowship, which consists in profession of doctrine and use of the Sacraments. For just as in Jacob's flock there are white and dark animals, sheep and goats [Gen. 30:32-40], in Peter's net good and bad [Mat. 13:47-48], lilies among thorns in the Lord's field [SSo. 2:2], tares among the wheat, Mat. 13:24 [-30], and grain with chaff on the Lord's threshing floor [Mat. 3:12], so in the visible church, insofar as it strikes the eyes, there are by outward profession not only believers and elect but also hypocrites, nonmalicious schismatics, nonmanifest heretics, impious, and sinners. Here belongs also the parable drawn from the dragnet, or fishnet, containing good and bad fish, Mat. 13:47, 49.

Thesis XVIII

And so the form of the church consists in unity of outward profession of the true doctrine, or in public fellowship of profession of the same faith and of public practice of the same.

Note: Though there are mixed among the good such as are wicked both as to doctrine and as to morals and life, yet by outward profession of doctrine and by participation of the same Sacraments they are consentient. Examples of this matter are set forth in 1 Cor. 10:18f. and 14:23f.

Thesis XIX

The true principal and essential marks of the church are the pure preaching of the divine Word and the proper [*legitima*] administration of the Sacraments, Eph. 2:19-20; John 10:26-27; Eph. 5:26-27; Mat. 18:20.

Note: The primary, unquestioned, and essential marks of the church militant on earth, by which it is surely and infallibly both recognized and pointed out to others and is distinguished from all other assemblies, are two: the pure preaching of the divine Word and the proper administration of the Sacraments. We prove this from the definition of the synthetic church, or [the church] taken collectively. For it is the assembly of people that embrace the Word of God and use the Sacraments, John 10:26-27: "My sheep hear My voice"; John 14:23: "If anyone loves Me and will keep My word" etc.; Eph. 5:25-26: "Christ loved the church, that He might sanctify her, cleansing [her] by the washing of water by the Word"; cf. Mat. 18:20. The most proper mark of the church is the true and pure preaching of the divine Word, to which the proper administration of the Sacraments in common is attached as virtually included in the profession of the truth—indeed a proper mark that belongs only to the true church, but not the whole [church] and always; for there once was the church before Abraham without the regular choreography of the Sacraments, and for 40 years in the desert the church did not observe circumcision. We therefore reject the false marks of the papists, of which Bellarmine lists 15.

Thesis XX

The one purpose of gathering and preserving the church is the highest, the other is subordinate. The highest is the glory of God, Eph. 1:11–12; the subordinate [is] the conversion and eternal salvation of people, 1 Ptr. 2:6; 5:10.

Note: The highest purpose of the church is the glory of God. For God gathers the church to this end, that He might have a special assembly by which He would be acknowledged, praised, and glorified, Eph. 1:11–12: "We have been called in Christ by a special choice [*sorte*]" (to heirship [*sortem*] or inheritance of the Lord), "that we should be to the praise of His glory." The subordinate purpose of the church is the turning of people from darkness to light, [their] translation out of the state of wrath into the state of grace, and [their] inheritance of eternal life. For "one who believes" in Christ, namely through the Word that is preached, "will not be put to shame," 1 Ptr. 2:6. Observe: This statement is found in Isa. 28:16 and is cited by Paul in Rom. 9:33 and 10:11 and by Peter in the passage cited. In Isaiah it is "לֹא יָחִישׁ, he will not run [away]." Caspar Sanctius, on Isa. 28, says that to be moved or to run [away] here is to feel ashamed. Now, in the passages cited the apostles followed the version of the Septuagint translators, who made it a practice sometimes to put what follows in the place of what precedes, so that it is "he will [not] become ashamed," that is, "he will [not] run [away] for shame." For they who are overcome with shame resort to flight and immediately withdraw themselves from the presence of people. The meaning therefore is: "One who believes will not run [away]," that is, one who will always have the failproof and everpresent remedy for evil in Christ will have no need to run away either out of very great anxiety or another fear of the heart. Observe, moreover: Isaiah simply says: "One who believes will not run [away]," but the Septuagint translators and Peter, who followed them, complete that [statement] by stating the object of faith: "One who believes ἐπ' αὐτῷ" (so also Paul, Rom. 9:33 and 10:11) "in Him." This προσδιορισμὸς [further definition] shows the connection of these words with the preceding promise of that corner- and foundation stone to be laid in the church; cf. 1 Ptr. 2:6.

Thesis XXI

The definition of the synthetic church is this: The synthetic church is the mixed assembly of people called and gathered, by the preaching of the Word and the administration of the Sacraments, out of the world to the kingdom of God and [to] participation of spiritual and heavenly blessings, who agree by outward profession of the true doctrine, for the praise of God and the eternal salvation of the very ones who are called.

Note: Gerhard states the form of the church in [his] definition of the church thus: "In this assembly are the elect, according to the foreknowledge [*praenotio*] of the Father, namely those who truly and perseveringly believe in Christ; with these are mixed the non-saints, but who nevertheless profess the same doctrine." And so He who calls or gathers the church is God; those who are called are the people; that by which they are called is the Word of God, the word of the Gospel; the starting point [from which they are called] is corruption and the state of wrath; the ending point is the kingdom of grace.

Thesis XXII

The attributes and adjuncts of the church are: Unity, catholicity, apostolicity, authority, visibility, splendor, affliction, [and] defectibility.

Note: The atributes and adjuncts of the church are:
1. Unity. For thus says the Constantinopolitan Creed: "I believe in one holy catholic and apostolic church." But this itself is to be understood not of some particular [church] but of the universal church as that which is in fact the spiritual body of Christ, 1 Cor. 12:27: "You are the body of Christ and members in part [KJV: in particular], ἐκ μέρους," so to say. Individually you are indeed members of Christ, yet your assembly does not complete [absolvit] His body, but only presents as it were a part in its own proportion. Luther well says: *"Ich glaube, daß eine heilige christliche Kirche sei auf Erden, das ist die Gemeine und Zahl oder Versammlung aller Christen, in aller Welt, die einige Braut Christi und sein geistlicher Leib, daß er auch das einige Haupt ist.* [I believe that there is a holy Christian church on earth, which is the communion and number or assembly of all Christians, in the whole world, the one bride of Christ and His spiritual body and that He is the only Head.]" The Apostles' Creed describes the unity of the church by κοινωνίαν ἁγίων, or communion of saints, by which, namely, the believers in Christ fellowship with Him and among themselves. And in what way this very thing takes place, the apostle explains in broader terms, Eph. 4:4, saying: "One body, and one Spirit, just as also you are called in one hope of your calling. One Lord, one faith, one Baptism, one God and Father of all," etc. In these words the apostle draws the basis of unity from the identity of the beginning, the middle parts, and the end, and teaches that the believers are united among themselves because they are ruled and moved by the same Holy Spirit by whom they have been called through the ministry of the Word to the same hope of salvation, because they have the same Lord and Redeemer, whose own they are, in whom they equally believe, and in whom they were at first implanted by Baptism, Rom. 6:5.

Finally, because they all have the same God and Father, "ἐξ οὗ πᾶσα πατρία ἐν οὐρανοῖς καὶ ἐπὶ γῆς ὀνομάζεται[after whom the whole family in heaven and on earth is named]," Eph. 3:15. The church is called "one" for this reason, that it is gathered by one God, is geared to one Head, Christ, embraces one doctrine, is reborn by one Baptism, is nourished by one body of the Lord, is ruled by one Spirit, is bound together by one bond of love, [and] aspires to and strives for one and the same inheritance, namely life eternal. Hülsemann says: "From this flow these two conclusions: (I) There is no one in the union and communion of the true church who lacks the influence of the sanctifying Spirit [and] who lacks the acknowledgement and confession of the same hope, the same Lord, the same faith, the same Baptism, and the rest of the requisites, [Eph. 4,] vv. 4-6. (II) Outward subjection under one shepherd or visible leader is not required for this unity by the teaching of the apostle." Cf. John 10:16; 11:52; 1 John 4:13. Irenaeus marvelously confirms this nature of unity, saying: "The church, though scattered throughout the whole world, carefully guarded this faith" (namely of the Apostles' Creed, which he had quoted), "as dwelling in one house, and held a unanimous belief regarding these things, as having one soul, Acts 4:32 [KJV], and preached and taught this faith with one voice, as each one having [all together] one mouth." But one should know that this part of the Constantinopolitan Creed, "I believe in one holy church," and especially that numerical word one, did not exist in the Apostles' or Nicene Creed, but was added only in the Constantinopolitan Creed, after the Arians, Novatians, Macedonians, Donatists, and similar heretics began to call also their conventicles churches. For this reason therefore, to distinguish by contrast the true church from assemblies given the same name, this mark of unity was inserted.

    2. Holiness, Eph. 5:27; 1 Ptr. 2:9. And it is called holy because it is called with a holy calling, because it is gathered under a holy Head, Christ, because it is a partaker of holiness, because it is made holy by the Holy Spirit, because it strives after holiness, and because it aims at perfect holiness.

    3. Catholicity, or universality. And the church is called

catholic (1) by reason of the evangelical doctrine, which always flourished, one and the same, in the church of God, Eph. 2:20 and Acts 15:11, and in this sense the church of both the Old and the New Testament can be called catholic; (2) by reason of place and duration, and in this way only the church of the New Testament is catholic. For it is scattered throughout the whole world, and it will remain until the end of the world.

4. Apostolicity. The church is called apostolic because it embraces the evangelical doctrine, taught by the apostles, according to apostolic understanding.

5. Authority, which indeed is great, but not greater than the authority of Holy Scripture.

6. Visibility. Because the ministry of teaching the Word and administering the Sacraments strikes the senses, therefore the assembly of the called is called the visible church; but because it is not visible to human eyes who then the true believers and the pious are in that assembly, therefore in respect to them the church is called invisible.

7. Splendor. The inner splendor of the church consists in faith and renewal; the outward [splendor consists] in the pure preaching and profession of the Word as well as the proper administration of the Sacraments, and because it contains the flower of the whole human race.

8. Affliction. For the church is for the most part subject to the cross, John 16:20; Acts 14:22; 2 Tim. 3:1.

9. Defectibility or deficibility. The catholic church together [*simul et semel*] has not erred even once in the foundation of faith, nor does it err, and it cannot end or be destroyed. Mat. 16:18: "You are Peter, and on this rock I will build My church, and the gates of hell [*inferorum*; lit. "of the inhabitants of the infernal regions"] will not prevail against it." With these words the firmness and the perpetuity of the church are promised, not [its] immutability and perpetual splendor, which the papists imagine. For the church can be firm and perpetual, because it is founded on a rock, though in this world its condition both changes from time to time and its appearance does not always seem the same. And "the gates of hell" here designates the

kingdom, force, power, and tyranny of the devil, or the vices, heresies, and persecutions that are stirred up by Satan, ruler of the inhabitants of the infernal regions, against the church. And so this is indicated, that no infernal might and power will prevail against the church of Christ and overcome it, but that it stands on the rock, Christ, unconquered until the end of the world. Moreover, the Savior speaks of the universal church. For the portals of hell prevail quite often against particular churches, as experience shows. For any particular church can err also in fundamentals, in fact defect, not only temporarily but also to the end. The promise of stability is indeed made also to particular churches, but with a certain condition, namely if they remain built on the solid rock, Christ, or if they do not depart from Christ, the rock of salvation, but adhere to Him in firm faith, or remain in His Word, John 8:31.

The Representative Church

Thesis XXIII

The representative church is called the assembly of the teachers and leaders of the churches, either of all or of individual ones, that represent the synthetic church and present a kind of an idea of it and make a compendium [of it].

Thesis XXIV

This assembly of teachers and overseers is otherwise called a council, in Greek σύνοδος [synod]; because this word also denotes any purely civic gathering of people consulting in common, the word *ecclesiastical* must be added.

Note: The whole visible church is represented in a meet and right council that presents some idea, as it were, of the whole church and makes a compendium [of it]. The derivation of the word [*council*] is drawn by some from divergent views to be reconciled [*conciliandis*], but that derivation is inadequate. More likely seems to be the one that is drawn from *concalando* [call together], or *convocando* [convoke] (hence *concilium* [assembly], as it were a called gathering for a festival and other things, as [derived] from καλέω [call]) or from the fixing and fastening [*intentione et conjunctione*] of the eyelids, i.e., of the eyes (Isidore: *supercilia* [eyebrows], because they are put above the eyelids, i.e., the eyes) in looking through a proposed matter. Its synonyms are σύνοδος [synod], or a gathering of many, [and] *Synedrion* [Sanhedrin], or a session of many, but the former word is used more often in Greek authors.

Thesis XXV

The principal and remote cause also of a particular meet and right council is God, Acts 15:28.

Note: Holy diets or councils have a divine origin. In the Old Testament: Num. 11:16; Deu. 17:9; Psa. 122:5. In the New Testament, as regards origin, Mat. 18:17; in [their] first form in that well-known apostolic assembly in Jerusalem, Acts 15:2[-22], where the first apostolic council is described, in which, as in a crystal-clear mirror the true form and by far the most beautiful pattern of a proper council is presented to us; from it also all other councils have taken [their] form, as Bellarmine himself confesses. And in this council at Jerusalem the highest leader was the Holy Spirit Himself; therefore it had [Him] as author.

Thesis XXVI

The proximate cause and handmaid that should assemble a council by public authority and set its place and time is the civil magistrate, Psa. 2:10[-12]; 24:7, 9; Isa. 49:23; Deu. 17:18; Rom. 13:1; 1 Ptr. 2:13; 2 Chr. 29:5, 21, 27, 30; 30:1, 6, 12; and he faithful and orthodox, 1 Cor. 6:1-2; or lacking such, the church itself, Acts 15:2[-29]; 20:28.

Note: Bellarmine indeed holds that the power to convoke and assemble councils, especially general councils, lies with the Roman pontiff. But we hold in general that the ordinary power to convoke councils and to specify time and place for a council lies with the civil magistrate. We prove this:

1. From the office of the magistrate regarding ecclesiastical matters; to this end God commends meditation in His law to the king, Deu. 17:18-19, etc. Also kings and princes, opposed to Christ and rebellious, are held by divine precept to kiss the Son, Psa. 2:10-12. The gates of the world are held to grant entry to the Lord of glory, Psa. 24:7, 9, etc.

2. We prove this from the practice of the ancient church. For the highest magistrat, i.e., the emperor, assembled or convoked ecumenical councils. Thus we know that those four ecumenical councils were assembled by emperors, namely [the council of] Nicaea by Constantine the Great, A.D. 325, against Arius, who denied the deity of Christ; Constantinople I by Theodosius the Great, A.D. 381, against Macedonius πνεθματομάχον [the Pneumatomachian[12]]; Ephesus I by Theodosius the Younger, A.D. 431, against Nestorius; and Chalcedon by Emperor Marcian, A.D. 451, against Eutyches. Hence Socrates says [in his] *Historia ecclesiastica*: "We mention the emperor for this reason, that, from the time of the first Christians, church matters depended on them, and so the greatest [*maxima*] councils (very many Latin editions read *maxime* [*especially* the councils]) were convoked, and still are convoked, according to their wish." Hence, when an opponent in a certain synod had condemned Hilary, Jerome

said: "I say that the emperor commanded this synod to be assembled." Cardinal Nicholas of Cusa also does not deny that eight ecumenical councils were convoked by emperors. And Marsilius of Padua proves from the proceedings of the councils that this constant freedom of action and power was only [that] of the emperors. And so to the outward ἐπισκοπὴ [supervision] of the civil magistrate belongs the responsibility to convoke, with power towards subjects, with comity toward aliens. The magistrate, I say, has power to convoke ecumenical councils if he is faithful and orthodox; but if not, the obligation to convoke does not therefore cease, if orthodox people demand it. In fact, when there is no faithful and orthodox magistrate, the church itself has power to convoke a council, either provincial or national or even universal, without harm to the lords of the territories from which the participants in the council are summoned. Or if the orthodox people cannot obtain the convocation of an ecumenical council from a heterodox magistrate and he fails in his office, the bishops themselves, according to the example of the apostles, as though by request, can assemble councils, yet not against the will of the lord of the territory. Thus Acts 15:2ff., when an argument arose in the church at Antioch about the need of circumcision and of the Law for salvation, the apostles and elders gathered a council to settle this controversy. Therefore, also the overseers are enjoined to take heed unto themselves and to the whole flock, Acts 20:28. And we know from church history that not only ecumenical but also μερικὰς [special] and τοπικὰς [local] or particular councils were convoked by emperors. In fact, we do not read that formerly also particular councils were assembled by primates or patriarchs, except at Rome. For everyone knows that there [at Rome] many councils were held at the call of its bishop, especially after the decline of the Roman empire and the establishment of the tyranny of the Antichrist. And likewise in Africa, where, it is clear from Augustine, the primates functioned in those roles. And if the primates and archbishops convoked councils, they did it not on their own authority but either on delegated [authority] or such as they assumed *de facto* [in fact], not *de jure* [by right].

Thesis XXVII (Lat.: XXVI)

The matter *ex qua* [of which (namely it consists)] of a council are the qualified persons who constitute the council and the consultants, the presiding officer, and the aides.

Thesis XXVIII (XXVII)

A presiding officer is required in a council for the sake of better order; and he is either the prince himself or his delegate, namely in a flourishing state of the church, or, if it is troubled, one or more to whom the church has entrusted this office.

Note 1: The right to preside in councils, especially general [councils], belongs to the highest magistrate. Now, by chairmanship or presidency we mean direction of the acts of a council that have regard not to τὰ ἔσω τῆς ἐκκλησίας, or the internal [matters] of the church, namely doctrine itself, but τὰ ἔξω, or the external [matters] and those that make for proper order. Therefore the ordinary chairman of the ecumenical and of the larger councils, with regard to external [matters] is the emperor or Christian prince and lord of the territory or someone sent or delegated by them. For a magistrate can delegate and assign his authority to bishops or others—not transfer [it] forever. The function of this civil chairman is to conduct by his authority the council assembled by him and to preserve inward and outward peace for those assembled and to provide safe conduct and see that all things are done in order and properly; to investigate the strifes and controversies that sometimes arise between bishops, to control disputes, approve the decrees of the greater and better party, [and] by public edict to sanction, confirm, and carry into execution the things that are approved.

Note 2: Moreover, among the bishops or by the emperor himself or by the prince or by common vote of the whole council he can be chosen who is to preside over the convention of a council and moderate τὰ ἔσω τῆς ἐκκλησίας, the inner [matters] of the church, or the ecclesiastical acts themselves that concern faith and doctrine. The functions of this ecclesiastical chairman are: to set before the whole council and clearly explain the state of the cause and of things to be discussed, to call the votes and conduct polls, hear others first, and then render a definitive judgment, draw up the decrees of the council and present them drawn up to the whole assembly for review and confirmation, and in the name of the council promulgate those that are then approved. Here one should note: (1) Already of old, this rank προεδρίας [of precedence] or of chairmanship was not local or bound precisely to one place or episcopate, but at large and left to the choice and judgment of the council of the Christian magistrate; this must be maintained over against the Roman pontiff, who holds that this προεδρία [chairmanship] perpetually belongs to himself. (2) The aforesaid functions of presiding were not always entrusted to some one bishop, but often more ecclesiastical chairmen were chosen in ecumenical and larger councils, who moderated the acts of councils either alternately or by working together, not by coactive but by ordinative authority. This is clear from the first apostolic council, Acts 15:7, 13, 19, 22 and from the practice and acts of the first four ecumenical councils. Therefore it is pure nonsense, contrary to right and observation, that the right of presiding over and of convoking councils belongs solely to the Roman pontiff, as we have fully shown [elsewhere].

Thesis XXIX (XXVIII)

Aides and competent judges, besides the chairman, are not only bishops but any faithful persons at home in the Holy Scriptures, both laymen and clergymen sent to the council by the churches, Rom. 14:12; 1 John 4:1; 1 Cor. 2:15; 10:15.

Note: Aides and judges in the councils, besides the chairmen are men of every rank, qualified and fit to judge. That is, not only bishops and presbyters, or teachers and pastors, to whom the ordinary supervision of the church and of religion has been entrusted, but also civil and lay people, as they are called, of good repute as to doctrine and knowledge of divine and ecclesiastical matters as well as piety, holiness of life, zeal for the truth, and acuity of judgment, delegated for that and sent to the council by their churches to compare views regarding that which is proposed. That is clear from the first apostolic council, in which there were not only the θεόπνεθστοι [divinely inspired] apostles but also presbyters and other pious men, both [men] familiar with the Antioch case and adjudicators and judges, Acts 15:6, 22–23, 25: "It seemed good to us, being assembled with one accord," etc. Verse 22 shows that the votes of all agreed with the statements of Peter and James. In Rom. 14:12 St. Paul says: "Every one of us is to give account of himself to God," especially at the time when he judges regarding the faith or an act of his brother. In 1 John 4:1 it is said to all believers that they should "test the spirits, whether they are of God." Cf. 1 Cor. 2:15; 10:15: "Judge what I say." Therefore the apostles admitted presbyters and other brothers, also laymen, to adjudication and to judge on the basis of the Holy Scriptures regarding the matter then set forth and discussed. The same was done in the church councils that followed, which not only bishops but also princes, presbyters, senators, judges, and other laymen not only attended but also acted in the interest of, deliberated, expressed views, [and] at the same time defined controversies and adjudicated [them] on the basis of Holy Scripture, as is to be seen in Eusebius, Sozomen, Theodoret, etc. Thus also Cyprian holds: "The matter of the lapsed is to be handled by discussion of the resolutions with bishops, presbyters, deacons, confessors, as well as laymen who are present." Also the adversaries accused of heresy are not excluded, as Eusebius says. Meanwhile it is enough for the judgment of laymen in the councils if they ratify what is decided by the teachers after sufficient declaration and possible discussion.

Thesis XXX (XXIX)

The matter *circa quam* [about which] or the object are [1] questions about doctrines and morals as well as [2] ceremonies in the church, Acts 15:19–20.

Note: The matter or object about which councils are concerned is in general holy and ecclesiastical matters that pertained either to faith, or life and morals, or also discipline and order in holy exercises to be performed; for example, in the first apostolic council, Acts 15:19–20, the question was about this article of faith, whether eternal salvation cannot be obtained without receiving circumcision and by observing the whole Law. (For, you see, controversy was stirred up for the apostles by pseudo-teachers not only about circumcision but about the whole Law.) The question was also about morals: whether it is necessary to abstain for a time from partaking of blood by obligation of the Mosaic ceremonial law or rather to avoid offending those who were converted from Judaism. Hülsemann well says: "That each object, both of faith and of morals, is appropriate for the investigation, discussion, and definition of the councils of the New Testament church, yet in such a way that they do not set forth any new article of faith besides that which is already set forth in the canon of the Holy Scriptures, is clear by induction of all the lawful councils and the acts in the same. And it is clear *a priori* from the rule of the apostle, Gal. 1:9.

Thesis XXXI (XXX)

The norm and principle of faith and decision in a council must be canonical Scripture alone, 2 Ptr. 1:19; Isa. 8:20; Gal. 6:16.

Note: The sole and sufficient norm according to which controversies are to be decided in councils is canonical Holy Scripture. For the prophetic and apostolic Word set down in writing is more certain than any other apparitions, and one should pay attention to it as to a light shining in a dark place, 2 Ptr. 1:19[–20]; Isa. 8:20: "To the law, rather, and to the testimony." Here the prophet sets the written Word of God as the ordinary, sure, and perpetual principle of things to be believed in contrast to superstitious investigations and all other means of searching for the truth; cf. Gal. 6:16. Therefore the decrees also of all general councils are to be tested and examined according to the touchstone of Scripture. To it also all council members in the primitive church conformed, according to the example of the apostles, Acts 15:15, and by it they condemned heretical errors as by the voice of the Spirit, the supreme judge of controversies. Alsted rightly says: "The first and last means that must be regarded in a council is Scripture, or rather God speaking in Scripture." And he would have this [to be] the practice of the ancients, who, in ecumenical councils, placed on a high throne in their midst a copy of the sacred and holy gospels as the sole foundation and principle of all Christian teaching and theological discussions. Dorsche says: "The custom observed by the following [after Nicaea] and by most of the councils, namely that Holy Scripture was placed in the midst, was followed also in the Council of Nicaea, in fact it is very probable that it flowed from the Nicene [council] into the others."

Thesis XXXII (XXXI)

The form is the order of a council, or the proper procedure with regard to the individual functions of the parties that are gathered.

Note: The form of a council is the proper order, or proper procedure, with regard to the individual functions and duties of the parties that are gathered; or rather it is that by which a church council is constituted and distinguished from other assemblies and that in it [i.e., in the council] judgment is undertaken regarding true and false religion, or discipline and ecclesiastical matters, according to the rule of the divine Word.

Thesis XXXIII (XXXII)

The goal of councils is the glory of God and the upbuilding of the church.

Note: This should be the goal, this the aim of all councils. First and foremost, the greatest care and concern to be brought to bear is that unity of faith be either restored or preserved and that strifes be ended. For councils, both ecumenical and particular, are assembled for these reasons:

1. That controversies about faith and religion that have arisen be adjudicated and settled by common effort; that heavenly truth and sincere religion be affirmed on the basis of the Scriptures; and that heterodox and heretical views be refuted, and that the heretics and schismatics themselves who are obstinate and incorrigible be condemned and repressed by public judgment.

2. If any corrupt practices have increased in the church, that they be terminated by common authority and consent.

3. That public scandals and blemishes be removed, and that εὐταξία [good order], order, and proper discipline be either established or preserved, canons or ecclesiastical laws regarding this matter having been established (for those that concern faith were included in the creeds, [and] those that concern discipline and morals [were included] in the canons or rules).

4. If there are any disagreements between pastors or even there is not the consensus that religion and love require, that they [the disagreements or differences] be removed in a proper council and thus, with scandals and offenses, which usually arise out of dissensions, removed from [their] midst, the peace of the church be guarded and unity and harmony be preserved and promoted.

Thesis XXXIV (XXXIII)

The definition of a council is this: An ecclesiastical council is an assembly of the whole church represented by its chief members, gathered by God through those to whom belongs the right to convoke, to deal, properly and according to the rule of the divine Word alone, with questions about doctrines and morals as well as ecclesiastical ceremonies, to the glory of God and the upbuilding of the church.

Note: Others define a council thus, that it is a public assembly set up and convoked either by a civil magistrate or by common consent of the churches, in which the teachers and pastors of the church, some also more-eminent civil servants, and other men endowed with pertinent gifts deliberate and, on the basis of Holy Scripture, resolve matters pertaining to the church, so that purity of the heavenly doctrine, uprightness of morals, and church discipline be affirmed and fostered and that evils, whether arising out of heresies and schisms or out of errors and abuses, be removed or guarded against.

Thesis XXXV (XXXIV)

There are different kinds of councils, as some are ecumenical, others national, others provincial, others diocesan. Ecumenical are [those] to the celebration of which learned and pious men are called out of all, or as many as possible, parts of the Christian world; and of this nature were the councils of Nicaea, Constantinople, Ephesus, Chalcedon, etc. National are [those] to which learned and pious men from one nation are summoned. Provincial, in which teachers of one province gather. Diocesan are [those] that consist of religious men of one diocese.

Note 1: Councils are divided (1) into canonical and ecclesiastical. We call [those] canonical that were held in the Old Testament by Moses, Joshua, David, Solomon, and other pious kings and one in the New Testament by the apostles, Acts 15. Ecclesiastical are [those] that were held in the church after the time of the apostles. [2] These [latter] are either [a] οἰκοθμενικὰ [ecumenical], universal, or general, which are assembled from the whole Christian world, or [b] μερικὰ [particular] and τοπικὰ [local], or particular, which are assembled in individual regions or provinces. In setting forth this division of councils, Augustine distinguishes between plenary councils and less full [councils]. Οἰκοθμενικὰ [ecumenical councils] are so called ἀπὸ τῆς οἰκουμένης [after the (Greek word for) world]; this word, taken in the wide sense, both in Greek and in Latin writers, denotes the Roman world or empire, as in Luke 2:1. If you take the former meaning οἰκοθμένης [of world], which denotes the whole habitable world, in that sense we never see an ecumenical council assembled. Therefore in terms of the latter meaning we see councils called ecumenical or universal, namely when learned and pious men are summoned and gathered from all or certainly most parts or churches of the Christian world who deliberate the most serious causes and controversies of the universal church and adjudicate them according to the rule of the divine Word. Such councils number mainly four: That of Nicaea, in which 318 bishops gathered, against Arius; Constantinople I, in which 150 bishops were assembled, against Macedonius; Ephesus I, in which more than 200 bishops came together and condemned the heresy of Nestorius; and that of Chalcedon, in which 630 fathers or bishops assembled, against Eutyches. To these four, three other universal synods are added, namely the Council of Constantinople II (under the guidance of which the already earlier Roman laws were reissued in one volume), called by Emperor Justinian in A.D. 553, in which the remaining ravings of Nestorius and Eutyches, as can be gathered from the confession of Emperor Justinian, were put to rest and the orthodox doctrine of the personal union, of the councils of Ephesus and Chalcedon, was set forth and confirmed. In this council also the errors of Origen were rejected, which [errors] found more than a few supporters in the East. The Council of Constantinople III, which was held A.D. 680 and 681, when Constantine IV was emperor, in which the heresy of the Monothelites, an offshoot of Eutychianism, was condemned. This synod is otherwise called Trullan and πενθέκτη, that is, quinisext, or fifth-sixth. The former name is from the place of the sacred palace that was called Trullus, the latter from the outcome, because this council adopted canons of the fifth ecumenical council. The Council of Nicaea II, in the year 787, convoked under Constantine and his mother Irene, against the iconoclasts, or destroyers of images.

Note 2: The lesser or particular councils, to the Greeks μερικὰ [particular] or τοπικὰ [local], are either national or provincial. They are called national when bishops and delegates of one people, nation, or realm gather in the good interest of their churches; very many of this kind were held of old in Africa, Asia, Spain, France, and other parts of the world. These are also called diocesan. For Constantine the Great reduced many provinces together into one body, as it were, or one diocese, which [provinces] were administered by one praetor of the vicars of the prefects. Those councils were also called national, plenary, or universal, likewise general, because they were general in that kingdom, not absolutely, as Bellarmine says. Provincial councils were [so] called from distinct provinces in one nation, namely when the bishops and presbyters of one province were gathered; for example, if from one province of Italy, like Tuscany, Lombardy, Liguria, etc. a Tuscan, Lombardic, or Genoan council is held; such councils in Germany were those of Mainz, Cologne, Aachen, and many others. In the Council of Toledo IV, held in the year 639, a third kind of particular councils was added that are called diocesan, under the jurisdiction of a diocese and its particular bishop, as Hülsemann says. And there are assemblies of the presbyters of one diocese under one bishop, or, as Bellarmine says, in which only the presbyters of one episcopate meet, and the bishop presides over them.

In passing, observe: the proceedings of all councils, both general and provincial, together with definitions and canons, gathered into one work, were first issued in 1538 by Peter Crabbe of Mechelen, a Franciscan, at Cologne. Soon after Peter Crabbe, after about 30 years, there was Lorenz Surius of Lübeck, a Carthusian, who, having gathered proceedings of councils from wheresoever and having added them to those already published, put together four volumes of them, issued likewise at Cologne in the year 1567. The edition of Surius was followed by one of Venice, a little larger, in the year 1575. Toward the beginning of the present century, namely in the year 1606, Severinus Binius, Doctor of Sacred Theology and professor in the school at Cologne, etc., issued a new edition, amplified beyond the earlier [editions] and embellished with dissertations and annotations. After two years, namely in the year 1608, there appeared by authority of the pontiff of Rome, from the Vatican press, the ecumenical, or general, councils, in Greek and Latin. Having obtained this, Binius prepared a truly large new edition in the year 1618. For besides other things, whatever is in that Greco-Latin [edition] he inserted in his edition. This, the very last edition of Binius, was reprinted in Paris in the year 1636 by Charles Morel, the king's printer, and divided into 10 tomes, which individually constituted practically a complete volume. In the preface the printer Morel promised two more tomes, which have not yet been issued, as far as I know. In the year 1671, under the direction of Philippe Labbe and Cossart, a complete edition of all councils, divided into 17 volumes, appeared. The Spanish councils of Garcia Loaysa and the English [councils] of Henry Spelman were put out in the year 1644 by the royal publisher; to these have been added the French councils of Jacob Sirmond, a Jesuit, in the year 1668. Stephan Baluze of Tulle issued the French councils of Narbonne and clarified [them] with notes. Bartolome de Carranza first issued Summa Conciliorum, printed repeatedly at Paris and elsewhere. Cariolanus Longius, a Capuchin, issued the Summa of Carranza in folio, enlarged and clarified with notes.

Notes:

1. *aggregatum.*
2. that is, the assembly that is gathered by the call.
3. or word; Lat. *vox.*
4. The Lat. word for him here is *praeco,* "crier, herald, preacher."
5. and in the wider sense: communion (as in "communion of saints," who are not all assembled at one place).
6. *terminus a quo,* "point from which."
7. *terminus ad quem,* "point to which."
8. *coetus,* or communion. See footnote 5 above.
9. From here on, *ecclesia* is generally translated "church."
10. *politicos.*
11. *catholica.*
12. This term implies, rightly or wrongly, that he held a false view of the Holy Spirit.

Section II: Polemic

Question I

Is the Church properly and principally the assembly of saints and true believers?

The Point at Issue

The question is not (1) whether there are hypocrites, evil people, and wicked people in the fellowship of the outward church. Nor is the question (2) whether the church is the assembly of only the elect, so that it consists of none but the elect, who only make and constitute the church, for also this, as a Calvinistic fabrication, we do not admit. Nor is the question (3) whether they who gather in Christian faith and in partaking of the Sacraments and in subjection to a proper pastor can in a certain sense be called members of the visible church; but this comes under investigation: Who then are to be considered true and living members of the church? Certainly in a sense we acknowledge only the truly pious and believers as true members of the church, but not all those who gather in profession of faith, partaking of the Sacraments, and in subjection to a proper pastor, as the papists would have it.

Thesis

The church, properly and principally, is the assembly of saints and true believers. But mingled with the outward assembly, which in a certain respect is and is called the visible church, are many unholy, hypocrites, and wicked, both by way of doctrine and of morals and life. But living, true, and properly so called members of the church are all and only believers, be they catechumens, or infirm in faith, or even excommunicated by the Roman assembly and curia.

Exposition

I. We do not deny that in this life many wicked and hypocrites are mingled with the saints in the outward fellowship of the church. Hence, since the Augsburg Confession, Art. VII, had said, "The church is the assembly of the saints, in which the Gospel is rightly taught and the Sacraments are rightly administered," Art. VIII adds: "Although the church properly is the assembly of saints, yet, since in this life many hypocrites and evil persons are mingled [therewith], it is allowable to use Sacraments administered by evil men."

II. The Apology of the Augsburg Confession, Art. IV, rightly [says]: "We grant that in this life hypocrites and wicked persons are mingled with the church and are members of the church according to the outward fellowship of the marks of the church, that is, Word, profession, and Sacraments."

III. One must distinguish between [1] the whole assembly of the called, or of those who are called through the Word to the kingdom of Christ and who obey this call, with regard to outward profession of faith, and [2] the assembly of the elect and of those who truly believe, [and] who adhere to Christ; evil persons and hypocrites are mingled with the former, not with the latter.

IV. Observe: They who are gathered by the call into the assembly of the church are of two different kinds: [1] Some are inwardly regenerated, renewed, and endowed with true faith by the Holy Spirit and in this way become true and live members of the church; [2] and some, lacking inner regeneration and holiness, associate themselves only by outward fellowship—which consists in profession of faith and use of the Sacraments—with the assembly of the called, or the church. The former are true and live members of the church, who draw life and breath from Christ the Head; the latter are putrid and dead. The former belong to the church inwardly, the latter only outwardly; the former without reservation, properly, and unequivocally, the latter in a certain respect, improperly, καταχρηστικῶς [by misuse of language] and ὁμωνύμως [equivocally]; the former in respect to inner and spiritual union with Christ, the latter in respect to outward association, profession, and fellowship with the assembly of the called; the former in the heart, the latter in outward appearance; the former in the judgment of God, the latter in the judgment of man; etc.

V. Observe: When some of those who hold our view say that the church is the assembly of the elect, then they do not use that term strictly and properly only for those who persevere in faith to the end of life, as Scripture defines the elect, nor do they use it in the Calvinistic sense for some elected by absolute decree of God, but in a wide and improper sense for all who are truly reborn, believe, and are holy; and so there is no difference between these two statements, that the church is the assembly of the saints and that the church is the assembly of the elect.

VI. We do not hold that there are two churches, one true, real, and inner, the other nominal and outward, but we say that one and the same church, namely the whole assembly of the called is considered in two ways, namely ἔσωθεν [inwardly] and ἔξωθεν [outwardly], or in respect to the call and outward fellowship consisting in profession of faith and use of the Sacraments, and in respect to inner regeneration and inner fellowship consisting in the bond of the Spirit. We grant that in the former way also hypocrites and unholy persons belong to the church, but we hold that in the latter way and respect only they who truly believe and [are] holy belong to it.

VII. One must distinguish between [1] the visible and particular church and [2] the invisible and universal church. In the visible and particular church the good and the evil, the elect and the rejected are mingled; but only the good belong to the invisible and universal church.

VIII. One must distinguish between [1] the church, called such without qualification, without saying whether it be true or false, when it is enough if it has the doctrine of the Gospel and the use of the Sacraments, though each [be] very corrupt, and [2] the church in particular, or the true [church], whose true and living members properly [so] called are all and only believers, be they catechumens, or weak in faith, or even excommunicated by the Roman assembly and curia.

IX. One must distinguish between the visible and the invisible church. Though hypocrites and secret heretics are obviously not members of the invisible church, yet they are members of the visible church, because of profession of faith, but dead [members], because of lack of regeneration and of faith. They are in the church but not of the church; they belong to the church in number, not justly, as Augustine says.

X. One must distinguish between [1] believers in general and in an improper sense, as opposed to all who are not baptized, unbelievers, pagans, Jews, and however many have not received faith in Christ; for these are said to be outside the church and not in it. And [2] believers in particular and in the proper sense, as opposed to all who are called Christian and have been received by Baptism but do not adhere to Christ in true faith.

XI. Observe: The nonbaptized are of two kinds: Some are altogether alien to the Christian religion and outside the church; but some, even though they have not received the Sacrament of Baptism, yet with inner and true faith kindled in their hearts by the Holy Spirit through the preaching of the Gospel, have the gift [of faith], like the thief on the cross, catechumens, martyrs carried away to death before receiving Baptism, and infants of Christians presented to Christ by the prayer of the church and of [their] parents—these, themselves not baptized, are living and true members of the church.

XII. One must distinguish between secret and manifest heretics. Secret heretics are also members of the church, though dead; manifest heretics are categorically not members, because they have separated themselves completely from the church. Thus also wicked schismatics are not members of the invisible church, yet they can be members of the visible church in part, though not completely.

XIII. One must distinguish between [1] those who are heretics in the judgment of the Roman curia, that is, of the Roman pontiff, and [2] those who are heretics in fact and in the judgment of God. The former, though they are excluded by their fellowship, that is, by the Roman Catholic church, are nevertheless not excluded from the true universal church, which includes all true believers.

XIV. One must distinguish between [1] members of the church by reason of inner form, namely faith and spiritual communion, and [2] members by way of outward profession of faith and outward use of the Sacraments. Not the former but the latter are members of the church as hypocrites, wicked, etc.

XV. Observe: They who are unjustly excommunicated as well as those who have been justly excommunicated but are penitent belong to the church triumphant, because they are of the number of those who are to be saved. Therefore they are also members of the church militant—if not of the visible [church], yet of the invisible.

XVI. One must distinguish between [1] sins of weakness, or of daily attack, as Tertullian calls [them], with which true faith and zeal for holiness can exist, and [2] sins against conscience, by which the reborn cease to be true and living members of the church.

Antithesis

I. Of the Audians, who, as Theodoret says, not only display great innocence of life but also admit only the chaste and holy to their fellowship.

II. Of the Novatians and Cathari (who line up under the banner of Novatus), in Epiphanius, who shut out of their fellowship those who had fallen in persecution, unwilling to receive them as penitents; this teaching is called καθαρόν [pure].

III. Of the Donatists, in Augustine, who hold that the church of Christ has perished from all the earth—because all in the whole world were infected by the contagion of sin—but remained with them alone.

IV. Of the Anabaptists, who deny that the assembly in which unholy are mingled is the true church and who hold that this church militant on earth is either no church or [is] holy, without wrinkle or spot.

V. Of the Puritans in England, who profess holiness of life as a mark of the true church and count themselves alone, above all people, to be the pure and holy church. Regarding the Puritans in England see John Laetus, who describes them excellently. "Such," writes James, king of England, "you may not without reason call our Puritan alchemic doctors of theology, with their quintessences of pure and purified doctrine."[1]

VI. Of the papists, like Bellarmine, as he criticizes this statement of the Augsburg Confession, Art. VII, that the church is the assembly of saints, who truly believe and obey God. "Now, our" (he adds, namely that of the Romans) "view is that the church is only one, not two, and that this one and true [church] is the assembly of people bound together by profession of the same Christian faith and fellowship of the same sacraments, under the rule of proper pastors and particularly of the one vicar of Christ on earth, the pontiff of Rome." But the view of the Lutherans, that the church in the proper sense is the assembly of saints, he says was put together from the heresy of the Pelagians, Novatians, and Donatists. The same papists categorically exclude catechumens or the unbaptized, heretics, schismatics, and the excommunicated from the church. For thus [says] Bellarmine: "Inasmuch as catechumens are not admitted to participation of the sacraments, they are excluded from the church." Again: "It is certain that catechumens are not actually and properly in the church, but only potentially." That heretics are not in the church is taught by Stapleton [and] Bellarmine. [And] Pistorius says that schismatics are not of the church. Bellarmine teaches the same. The Roman Catechism [says the same] regarding those who are excommunicated, namely that they are not in the church.

VII. Of the Labadists, who hold that all modern churches are completely corrupt [and] that only the Labadic assembly consists of true believers and the best teachers.

Confirmation of the Thesis

We prove our view, namely that the church is properly the assembly of saints, from the nature and character of the true church. For in Holy Scripture the church is called

I. The mystical body of Christ, Rom. 12:5; 1 Cor. 10:17; 12:27; Eph. 1:23; Col. 1:18. And they who are not dependent on the Head, Christ, do not have spiritual life, motion, and operation, that is, they are neither enlivened nor ruled by the Holy Spirit; they are not true and genuine members of that mystical body, namely the church. Hence we conclude: "The church is the body of Christ, whose individual members, among themselves mutually συμβιβαζόμενα [held together] καὶ συναρμολογούμενα [and joined] by the power of the Head, work and grow with the increase of God, to the upbuilding of its body in love, Eph. 4:16; Col. 2:19. The assembly of saints and of true believers is such a body. Therefore the assembly of saints and of true believers is the church." That is a true member in any body, which receives motion, life, and feeling from the head and which in turn is connected through participation of the spirit, life, and feeling. Now, only true believers, etc. Ergo. The minor [premise] is proved from Eph. 1:4-5.

II. The church is the mother not of the dead but of the living, or of true believers, Gal. 4:26. They who are born of God are sons of God and spirit of the Spirit, John 1:12[-13]; 3:6. They are led by the Spirit of God, Rom. 8:14; and therefore they put to death, by the Spirit, the works of the flesh, v. 13; they are heirs of God and joint heirs with Christ. It is clear that these properties of the sons of God do not hold for all the called who are in the outward fellowship of the church. Therefore not all the called belong to the assembly of the sons of God, that is, to the church properly and principally so called.

III. The church is the sheepfold of Christ, John 10:1, and the true citizens of the church are also the sheep of Christ. Moreover now, the sheep of Christ hear the voice of Christ, their Shepherd, and Christ knows them; they follow Christ, their Shepherd, and Christ gives them eternal life, and no one snatches them out of the hands of Christ, John 10:27-28. This description does not fit all who are in the outward fellowship of the church, but only true believers. To the sheepfold of Christ belong only sheep, because it is αὐλὴ τῶν πρωβάτων [a sheepfold], v. 1. And the wicked are not sheep, but goats, etc.

IV. The prophets and apostles often bestow praises on the church, [e.g.,] Psa. 45:13 [and] SSo. 4:7, which cannot be applied to the whole assembly of the called, which includes good and evil, wheat and tares, Mat. 13:24[-30], good and bad fish, sheep and goats, Mat. 3:12; 13:47, 49; John 10:1[-29]. Therefore one must envision some true church, properly and κυρίως [correctly] so called, to which those praises and attributes πρώτως [primarily] and ἀμέσως [directly] belong. For here and there in the Old and New Testament it is called the bride of Christ, SSo. 4:8-10; Isa. 61:10; Hos. 2:19-20; John 3:29; 2 Cor. 11:2; Rev. 21:9. The bride of Christ is all fair, SSo. 4:7; a pure virgin, 2 Cor. 11:2; and one flesh with Christ, like wife and husband, Eph. 5:30. None of these things squares with the wicked. The house of the living God, 1 Tim. 3:15. A spiritual building, 1 Ptr. 2:5; Tit. 2:14-15. None belong to this except those who are living stones, built on the chief cornerstone, Jesus Christ, Eph. 2:20-21; 1 Ptr. 2:5.

V. Bad fluids are not parts of a body. The wicked are like bad fluids. Therefore they are not parts of the body, namely of Christ, but they cling to the church, like ulcers to a body, and they can be separated from it without harm, in fact with great benefit of the body.

Catechumens endowed with true faith are true members of the church (1) because they are saved. Bellarmine himself admits the premise [*assumptum*] and proves it from the oration of Ambrose on the death of Valentinian. For no one is saved except one who is actually in the church. Outside the church there is no salvation. (2) No one can have God as Father who does not have the church as mother. Faithful catechumens have God as Father. Ergo. For all believers are children of God, John 1:12; Gal. 3:26. (3) They who are members of Christ, they also are members of the church. Faithful catechumens are members of Christ, for all believers are in Christ, for faith implants in Christ, makes members of Him.

They who are unjustly excommunicated do not cease to be members of the universal church, even though they are put out of the visible and particular church. We prove this (1) from Luke 6:22. You are blessed ὅταν ἀφορίσωσιν ὑμᾶς [when they exclude you]. Therefore some are and remain blessed also after separation and excommunication. But no one can be blessed unless he be a true and living member of the universal church. (2) From John 16:2, where Christ says to His disciples: "They" (the high priests of the Jews) "will put you ἀποσυναγώγους [out of the synagogues]"; cf. John 9:22, 24, namely because of the confession of Christ. However, the apostles did not cease to be members of the church by such excommunication. (3) No one is saved who is not a member of the church. Some who are excommunicated are saved, namely (a) they who are unjustly excommunicated [and] (b) they who are indeed justly excommunicated but repent and die before public absolution. (4) They who are of the spirit of the church, they are in fact members of it. If they who are excommunicated have faith and love, they are of the spirit of the church, as Bellarmine says. Therefore, if they who are excommunicated have faith and love, they are in fact members of the church. (5) One to whom the way is open to the church triumphant, he is clearly not separated from the church militant. When they who are excommunicated are penitent and die in this state before public absolution, the way is open to them to the church triumphant. Ergo. The proposition is proved by words of Bellarmine, who says: "The church triumphant is united, in fact it is rather one with the [church] militant, and therefore no one can be willing to be separated from the one unless he is separated from the other."

Vindication

To our first proof, Bellarmine replies: "The wicked are dead and dry members, yet, in spite of this, true members of the church." We reply: Just as a painted man is only ambiguously called a man, so dry and dead members are only ambiguously members. In Eph. 1:23 the church is called not only the body of Christ but also πλήρωμα, the fullness of the body; however, dry and dead members do not fulfill or complete a body but rather burden it. In Eph. 4:16 the whole body of the church is called properly joined and put together by what every joint supplies, according to the power working within, in keeping with the measure of every member; but this cannot be said of dry and dead members, for they are not joined to the body by the spirit of life; there is no ἁφῆ [connection] or ἐνέργεια [energy] in them; the same are also not able to grow. In Col. 2:19 it is said of this mystic body, that by joints and connections supplied and put together it grows with the increase of God. Now, dry and dead members are neither joined to the other members of the body, nor do they grow with the increase of God, etc. Therefore true and living members of Christ and of the church are not they who are not ruled by the Spirit of Christ.

To the second proof, namely that the true members of the church are also sons of God, etc., Bellarmine replies: "The word 'son' is taken in three ways: (1) in the way of production; (2) in the way of imitation; (3) in the way of teaching. The wicked are sons of God, not indeed by way of regeneration but rather by way of teaching, and that is enough so that they might be called sons of the church." We reply: When it is said that they who do not have God as Father do not have the church as mother, that is to be understood of sons who are such by regeneration, not only by teaching; for they who are sons neither by regeneration nor by imitation but only by teaching, they are sons of the devil, but not sons, properly so called, of God and of the universal church.

As to the third proof, that the true citizens of the church are also the sheep of Christ, Bellarmine objects: "'Sheep' is sometimes taken indiscriminately, both for good and for bad, as in John 21:16, 'Feed My sheep,' sometimes only for the predestined, as in John 10:27, 'My sheep hear My voice.'" We reply: It is enough that he concedes that in John 10:27 this word is taken only for the predestined, for in v. 16 it is added, "There will be one flock and one shepherd." Therefore only the predestined belong to the flock of the universal church.

As to the proof regarding catechumens, Bellarmine replies: "Catechumens are in the church, if not actually and in fact, yet potentially, by devout wish and desire, and that suffices them unto salvation." We reply: It is certain that as many as are saved, they are of the church not only by devout wish and potentially but also in fact and actually; for none are saved unless they are first actually called out of the world into the church; none are saved unless they are first implanted in Christ by faith; and he that through such a call actually passes over into the church and he that through faith becomes a member of Christ, he is actually in the church. Just as no one could have been saved in the Flood unless he was actually in the ark of Noah, so also can no one be saved unless he is actually in the church. Bellarmine replies: "Comparisons do not apply at all." But they necessarily apply in the point of comparison at which the comparison is drawn. Now, the church is compared to the ark of Noah in this particular respect, that no one is saved outside the church just as no one outside the ark was kept safe and sound from the waters of the Flood.

As to them that are excommunicated unjustly, Bellarmine objects: "It suffices them unto salvation that they are in the church by desire and in spirit." But this reply does not suffice. For no one is saved unless he is indeed and actually of the church, as aforesaid. They that are excommunicated unjustly are actually and indeed members of Christ. Therefore they are also actually and indeed members of the church. Bellarmine says: "Outward communication properly makes a person [part] of the visible church." So he tacitly concedes that excommunication does not separate a person from the number of the saved but from the visible church. He therefore in fact concedes that excommunication does not separate from the universal and invisible church, outside of which no one is to be saved and within which are all who are to be saved.

Refutation of Objections

I. Bellarmine counters with the parables of the gospels drawn from the threshing floor on which both wheat and chaff were put, Mat. 3:12; from the dragnet or fishnet containing good and bad fish, Mat. 13:47, 49; from the wedding banquet to which good and bad are called and come, Mat. 22:10, 12; from a sheepfold in which are sheep and kids or goats, John 10:1[-16]; from the ten virgins, etc. We reply: Those parables point out two things: The one, that in the outward fellowship and life, bad are mingled with the good; because of hypocrisy the bad cannot always be easily discerned nor separated from the pious in this world. The other, that though that kind of persons thrust and intermingle themselves in outward fellowship, yet they are not true members of the church. For the chaff is burned up with fire, the bad fish are discarded, the guests who lack a wedding garment are cast out, the goats are consigned to hell, the virgins who lack oil are shut out. It is not true to say this of the true members of the church.

II. He counters with "some passages and examples that point out that great sinners are often found in the true church." We reply: The pious are also subject to failures and are sometimes carried astray by the lust of the flesh and fall into sins, but they do not cling to them and do not therefore immediately lose membership in the church. But they who persist in sins, they drop out of the number of sheep of Christ and pass over to the goats. They are in the church but not of the church, etc. The papists insist: "The Lord tolerates the unfruitful fig tree in His garden, that it might bear fruit, Luke 13:6[-9]. Paul calls the assembly of the Corinthians 'church,' though there were fornicators, contentious, [and] proud in it, 1 Cor. 1:11 and 3:3; 5:1[-13]. Paul honors the assembly of the Thessalonians with the name 'church,' though there were in it those that walk disorderly, 2 The. 3:6," etc. We reply: By those examples of the unfruitful fig tree, the Corinthian church, the Thessalonian [church], etc., nothing else is proved than that good and bad are found in the outward fellowship of the church, which we readily admit, but that unbelievers and hypocrites, who only profess faith with the mouth, are true and living members of the church cannot be proved by the passages cited.

III. He objects: "All who are baptized are called sheep and children of God, though there still are many among them who lack the Spirit of Christ and true love according to the statements in 1 Cor. 12:13, 'We are all baptized into one body'; Gal. 3:27, 'As many [of] you [as] have been baptized have put on Christ.'" We reply: They who have been baptized are living members of the true church so long as they lead a life worthy of Baptism, Rom. 6:3-4. Even Simon Magus was baptized, yet no one regarded him as a citizen and son of God, Acts 8:20-21ff. Therefore one who has put on Christ is a citizen of the church as long as he is not cut off, by a sinful life and faithlessness, from the vine, Christ, in whom he was implanted as a branch, John 15:1[-6].

IV. The papists argue on the basis of 1 Cor. 10:17: "'We, being many, are one bread, one body, for we all partake of one bread'; now, also the wicked eat the sacramental bread; therefore they are one body with the others, [who are] believers." We reply: (1) Cornelius a Lapide and Estius note on this passage: This does not speak of the unity among themselves of those who commune, but [of their unity] with Christ (which one gathers from the preceding verse 16 and the following verse 18). Moreover, even the papists themselves concede that clearly the wicked do not receive an influx from the Head, Christ. [2] Hence Cyprian argues the opposite way on the basis of this passage: "As the chaff does not enter the bread, so are the reprobate not true parts of the church that is called one bread."

V. Bellarmine argues: "The church that Paul persecuted was either the true church or a false church. If [it was] the true [church], then Paul was never a member of the true church, for how was he [a member] of the church that he opposed with all his might? If that was not the true church, then Paul and Luke lie when they catagorically call it the church of God." We reply: We speak of the predestined [who are] actually already called. Bellarmine himself distinguishes between sheep of Christ and members of the church according to predestination and according to present righteousness and says: Sheep or sons or members according to predestination are not actually but only potentially such, but [they who are] such according to present righteousness, they are such actually and absolutely. Therefore, when the universal church is called the assembly of the elect, it is properly understood in the latter sense; they who are thus called elect according to [their] present state are actually and absolutely members of the universal church; but the elect according to foreknowledge are called members of the church, not actually [such] but by the potential [that is] to be brought in due time into reality, and in a certain respect.

VI. Observe: All hearers are said to be elected [Ger. *Auserwehlte*] by pastors, not that all [are] holy or elected to eternal life, but because they [are] singled out, separated from the assembly of the faithless and chosen for the kingdom of grace.

VII. One must distinguish between [1] true and living members of the church, who draw life and spirit from Christ, the Head, and belong to the true church, and [2] putrid and dead members, which are to be cut off from the body of the church. Likewise, one must distinguish between [1] a dead and [2] a weak member of the church. Someone can be a weak member of the church, like a hand, weak in a body, for example, which [member] is nevertheless not yet a dead member but still has life and spirit, though weak.

VIII. One must distinguish between [1] being in the church, 1 Cor. 11:19; 2 The. 2:4, which is nothing else than to live in the assembly of those who, as regards the preaching of the Word and the administration of the Sacraments, constitute the true church, even as to be in the world, John 17:11, is to live among the children of this world; and [2] being of the church, which is clearly to concur with the doctrine of the Word and of the Sacraments, just as to be of the world is to follow and approve the wicked ways of the world.

IX. One must distinguish between [1] being a part of the church and [2] being a member of the church. To be a part is more general and refers to a whole something; in this sense they who are not holy are and can be called true parts of the church because they live and are active as it were in its bosom, just as, on the other hand, the pious who are attached to a false and heretical church can also be called parts of it as long as they continue in its outward fellowship. But to be a member is more intimate and has reference to a living body or at least refers to something similar and analogous. The wicked and hypocrites can indeed be called parts of the true church, but in no way members properly [so] called.

X. One must distinguish between [1] an outward influx, which takes place by way of prevenient grace, and [2] inner [influx], which takes place by means of indwelling grace. The former does not yet constitute [one] a member of the church, but by it [one] first begins to become a member of the church; however, the latter does constitute [one] a member, and where that [is], there [is] finally a true and real member of the church.

XI. One must distinguish between the parts of the church [1] insofar as they are considered as members and [2] insofar as [they are considered] as instruments. One can be in the body of the church by way of an instrument, yet so that it is not yet by way of a member. Thus among the parts of the church are listed also ministers [who are] hypocrites and of a wicked life, through whom Christ acts as through instruments, who nevertheless are not true members of the church, because they do not have vital influx from Christ; see 1 Cor. 12.

XII. As to catechumens, Bellarmine counters with the passage in Acts 2:41: "They that received the Word [were] baptized"; and likewise the Council of Florence and the fathers who teach that people become members of Christ and of the body of the church when they are baptized. We reply: (1) Though the outward fellowship of some particular church may be entered by baptism, as that of Jerusalem, Acts 2, yet [it is] by faith [that] aggregation takes place into the universal church, outside of which there is no salvation. (2) Though also in ancient times there was a difference between catechumens and the faithful, yet all understood that those were called faithful in the strict sense who were more perfectly informed in all chief parts of the Christian faith.

XIII. Bellarmine objects: "One who is excommunicated is regarded as a heathen; but heathen are not of the church." We reply: We do not fight for those who are justly excommunicated and persevere in their obstinacy; but it is not a valid line of argument that leads from these to those who are either struck by an improper sentence of excommunication or repent and so die.

XIV. He objects further: (1) By excommunication people are deprived of all spiritual relations that the people of the church have among themselves. (2) Excommunication has the place in the church that the death penalty has in the temporal state. (3) Excommunication is the greatest penalty that the church can impose. (4) The apostle himself says of one who is to be excommunicated, 1 Cor. 5:13: "Put away from yourselves the wicked one"; therefore excommunication is expulsion from the church, and therefore one who is excommunicated is not of the church. We reply: One must distinguish here between (1) [a] one who is deservedly excommunicated and [b] one who is undeservedly [excommunicated], (2) [a] one who repents and desires to be freed from the sentence of excommunication and [b] one who obstreperously defies [it], (3) [a] the bosom and embrace of the universal church and [b] the lap or fellowship of some particular church, [and] (4) [a] outward and [b] inner fellowship. By unjust and undeserved excommunication, or that which takes place by an erring key, nothing of that right is lost to one who is excommunicated, which is his unto eternal life as a faithful member of Christ.

Notes:

[1] *Huiusmodi Puritanos nostros non iniuria chymicos Theologiae Doctores appelles, cum suis illis purae & purgatae doctrinae quintis essentiis.*

Question II

Is the church rightly distinguished into visible and invisible?

The Point at Issue

The question is not (I) whether there is any given visible church in the world; nor (II) whether the church, with regard to outward confession of faith and use of the Sacraments and of other pious exercises that strike the outward senses, can and should be regarded as visible; nor (III) whether there is given a double church, distinct in species, the one visible, the other invisible. But (IV) this is the question: Is the church, with its unity intact, variously considered, rightly divided into a visible and an invisible [church]?

Thesis

The church, with its unity intact, variously considered, is rightly divided into a visible and an invisible [church]. With regard to the called, the church is called visible; with regard to the elect [it is called] invisible; however, the invisible [church] is not to be sought outside the visible church, but the former is included in the latter.

Exposition

I. Observe: We do not introduce two churches ἀντιδιῃρημένως as opposed to each other, so that the visible and invisible churches would be contradistinct species, but we call the one and the same church visible and invisible in a different respect: visible in respect to the called, invisible with respect to the elect.

II. One must distinguish between [1] the church seen in itself, which is one and the same and remains at all places and times, and [2] various ways, relations, and respects of considering it, which neither constitute various species of it, nor are they set contrary or contradictory, but they are subalternate and subordinate in such a way that the invisible church of the elect is contained in and under the visible assembly of the called. And as the elect are not to be sought outside the assembly of the called, so also [is there] no invisible [church] outside the visible church.

III. One must distinguish between [1] the various significations and meanings of a word that contain the difference of an equivoque in its equivocate[1] and [2] the division of a matter into distinct and disjunct species, or churches opposed to each other, so that the one would be visible, the other invisible—which never entered anyone's mind.

IV. One must distinguish between [1] the church considered in general for the common assembly of all who are called by the preaching of the Word and who use the Sacraments, and as long as this remains such it is visible, and [2] the church seen in particular as the assembly of the elect, comprehended in that general assembly that properly is invisible. People indeed are seen who belong to the kingdom of Christ, yet they are not seen surely and distinctly in that they belong to it.

V. One must distinguish between the outward and the inner form of the church. The former consists in the well-ordered, outward, local, manifest, and visible assembly of many, or in the public profession of the same faith and the use of the same Sacraments. The latter [consists in] spiritual, inner, hidden, and invisible fellowship; and it is the union and joining together of the faithful in one Spirit, through the same faith and mutual love under one Head, Christ, and it simply is of the essence of the church.

VI. One must distinguish between [1] the flourishing state of the church, when the Word is publicly preached and the Sacraments administered without hindrance, and [2] the state [of the church] under pressure, when outward profession is sometimes hindered by the cruelty of tyrants and other causes and it is so oppressed by troubles and persecutions, so beclouded by offenses, so reduced to few in number, that it cannot become visible to the individual members themselves of the same particular church, much less to a whole province or to other churches, and then the church is also rendered invisible or not evident to the eye.

VII. Hence it is clear that we say that the church is visible not only in name and ἀλληγορικῶς [allegorically], as the papists charge, but truly and in fact.

VIII. We do not speak here only of the church triumphant—which not even the papists themselves can deny to be invisible to human eyes not yet enlightened—but also of the church militant on earth.

IX. We do not deny that when, in the Last Judgment, Christ will separate the sheep from the goats and set the elect at [His] right hand, Mat. 25:32, then the universal church, which is the assembly of the saints, will be visible and evident to the eyes, but here we speak of the church considered in the state of this life.

X. In the question about the visibility of the church, the adversaries change the point of the question, for they deal with us as though we recognize no visible church. We could not be farther from that view. But we say that the church of the elect is now invisible and that it will not be visible until Judgment Day. For election is not perceived with the eyes or discerned by sight.

Antithesis

I. Of the papists, who call the invisible church allegorical, phantom, imaginary, utopian, Platonic ideas, metaphysical, etc.

Bellarmine says: "The church is an assembly of people, visible and palpable, just as is the assembly of the Roman people or the kingdom of Gaul or the republic of Venice." And: "Not even one passage can be cited in which the name 'church' is attached to an invisible assembly." And: "The Lutherans say that the true church is invisible and known only to God. We affirm the contrary." Stapleton [says]: "The true and universal church is a multitude dispersed throughout all peoples. But the elect, as Christ says at the end of the parable in Mat. 20:16, are few. Therefore the elect, as such, do not constitute the true church, but as visible and called, and consequently the distinction between the visible and the invisible church is false." Therefore the papists reject the distinction of the church into visible and invisible, recognizing no invisible church, and they hold that the elect, as such, do not constitute the true church, but as visible and called.

II. Of the Weigelians, who hold that the true church is indeed dispersed throughout the whole world but that it is not found in any specific place and visible assembly; or that the church is not visible but invisible, because it is not bound to any one place but [is] spread throughout the whole world.

Confirmation of the Thesis

The thesis is proved

I. By clear words and statements of Scripture in which the church is described (1) by [its] inner splendor and glory, Psa. 45:13; Rom. 2:28–29; 1 Ptr. 3:4. Now, these praises do not belong to the visible church; it is therefore necessary that besides this there be some invisible church; here see especially the Song of Solomon. The line of thought is this: That which is hidden is invisible; the church κατὰ πρῶτον λόγον [according to the first term] is invisible. (2) The church is described as a mystical body and a spiritual kingdom, whose Head and Lord is Christ, who, since He is invisible, 1 Ptr. 1:8, also ought to have members similar to Himself. (3) Knowledge of those who are true and living members of the church belongs to God alone, 1 Kin. 19:18; Rom. 11:4; 2 Tim. 2:19: "The Lord knows those who are His." These God has sealed with the Spirit of adoption, 2 Cor. 1:22; Eph. 1:13; 4:30. "And He gives them a white stone, on which [is] written a name that no one knows except the one who receives [it]," Rev. 2:17. Now, if [it is] visible only to [the eyes] of God but not to [those] of human beings, namely who the true and living members of the church are, certainly also the true church is invisible.

II. By reasons, of which (1) [is]: Because the catholic church, as such, is something universal. Now, universals, insofar as they are universals, are an object of reason or of faith, not of sense [perception] or of the eyes, and so they are not felt with the hands or seen with the eyes but are either known or believed. (2) Because its form [is] inner and essential, which is spiritual communion and faith, it cannot be seen or perceived by the eyes of the body. (3) Because its members also as to their outward form or material cannot be seen all together and all at once by any one individual or even by many, because of the remoteness of the places. (4) Because the outward form, because of tyrants or the neglect and wickedness of human beings, can be so impeded or lost that it becomes invisible to the eyes of the body. (5) Because the church is properly described according to the part [that is] both greater and stronger, and the part of the church [that is] both greater and stronger is invisible, it is therefore called invisible. The minor [premise] is proved both [a] by the church triumphant, which, as Bellarmine says, is not united with but one with the church militant, but this [church triumphant] itself, as the stronger and greater part of the church, is invisible, and [b] by the assembly of the elect, which cannot be discerned by the sight of the eyes. (6) Because what is seen is not spiritual. Now, the church is spiritual and an object of faith, 1 Ptr. 2:5 and according to the Apostles' Creed. Hugh of St. Victor rightly [quotes] from St. Augustine: "If you see [it], then it is not faith." (7) Because, if there were no church except one that is seen by the eyes of human beings, it would have perished at the time of the Baal idol madness. But it did not perish. Therefore there is a church that is not seen by the eyes of human beings. The major [premise] holds, because the prophet Elijah, 1 Kin. 19:10, 14, laments that he alone was left. The minor [premise is established] by this, that in the same chapter, verse 18, God says that He had left seven thousand men who had not bowed their knees to Baal.

Vindication

Bellarmine does not attack our stronger arguments, with which we prove that in a certain sense and respect the church is invisible; he cites some weaker [arguments] and tries to reply to them; to these objections Gerhard replies at length. We [reply] briefly: When we say that the kingdom of God is spiritual and prove that from Luk. 17:20, "The kingdom of God does not come μετὰ παρατηρήσεως, with observation," and verse 21, "The kingdom of God is within you," Bellarmine objects: "By 'kingdom of God' is meant either grace, by which God rules in the hearts of human beings, as Theophylact explains [it], or Christ Himself, as Bede explains [it]." We reply: We accept the interpretation of Theophylact, which confirms our view, for, you see, it is not clear to human eyes in whose hearts Christ dwells and rules by grace in them. Now, the Savior wants to say: The kingdom of God does not come μετὰ παρατηρήσεως, with observation, that is, with outward splendor and magnificent display, like the kingdoms of this world, but it is a spiritual and inner kingdom, whose beginnings, progress, and increases are hidden to the eyes of human beings. But how does the statement of Bellarmine, that the church is an assembly of human beings, [and] thus visible and palpable, as is the assembly of the Roman people or the kingdom of Gaul, etc.—[how does this] mesh with this statement of Christ? It certainly cannot be denied that these kingdoms come with observation, that is, outward splendor, etc.

When we prove that the church is a spiritual house from 1 Ptr. 2:5, where Peter [says]: "You yourselves, as living stones, are also being built up a spiritual house, a holy priesthood, bringing spiritual sacrifices acceptable to God through Jesus Christ," Bellarmine replies: "Something is called spiritual in two ways: in one way according to substance, in which way the angels are called spiritual, [and] in the other way according to ordering with regard to spirit, as the body is called spiritual and good works are called spiritual sacrifices. The church is called a spiritual house in the second way, since the apostle means that the church is a house built not of wood and stones but of human beings consecrated to God." We reply: We agree that the house of the church is built of spiritual human beings, that is, reborn by the Spirit of God; now, because they are seen as corporeal human beings, but not as spiritual human beings belonging to the house of the church, therefore it still remains firm that the church as a spiritual house built of spiritual human beings is invisible. Human beings become the spiritual house of God and true members of the church alone by the regeneration and renewal of the Spirit. But now, that operation of the Spirit is inner and in no way set forth [before] the eyes of human beings, 1 Cor. 2:11. Therefore also it cannot be seen, then, which human beings are truly spiritual.

In the Apostles' Creed we confess that we believe in the catholic church; therefore we do not see it. Bellarmine here twists variously; (1) he replies: "It is not only stated in the Creed, 'I believe in the church,' but 'I believe in the holy church'; now, the holiness of the church is doubtless invisible." But he himself abandons this reply and rightly, for we both confess that we believe that there is a church and that it is holy. If only the holiness of the church but not the church itself were the article of faith, then one would have had to say, "I believe in the holiness of the church," and not "I believe in a holy church." [2] He therefore adds another reply, namely: "In the church something is seen, namely an assembly of human beings, and something is believed, namely that this assembly itself is the true church of Christ, which professes faith in Christ." Coster makes the same reply, and Becanus repeats [it]. We reply: What Bellarmine says, that we also say in every respect. For we see an assembly of human beings, which is the church, but we do not see whether those human beings are the church, that is, the human beings who belong to the church are seen and observed, but that those human beings are true and living members of the church does not appear outwardly.

Refutation of Objections

I. Bellarmine objects: "Not even a single passage can be cited in which the name 'church' is attached to an invisible assembly, but wherever the name 'church' occurs, it always means a visible assembly." We reply: (1) Wherever the name "church" is taken properly and specifically and is put for the catholic church it denotes the invisible assembly of the saints and of the true believers, because none are true members of the catholic church except true believers and saints, as so often said. (2) That the invisible church must be understood is proved by those outstanding eulogies and praises that are found added. (3) Mat. 16:18: The gates of hell will not prevail against the church built on the rock; but the gates of hell often prevail against visible churches in particular. (4) The same church is meant in the Scriptures as is set forth in the Creed; now, in the Creed such a church is meant as is not seen but which is believed: I believe in the catholic church. Very many passages that Bellarmine amasses here to deny the invisible church speak of particular assemblies; no one denies that they are visible and strike the eyes; some also speak of the catholic church, which is the invisible assembly of the saints, like the passage in Mat. 16:18.

II. Bellarmine counters with the passage in Psa. 19:4: "He has set His tabernacle in the sun." The same [Bellarmine] says: "Just as the sun can certainly not be concealed, so also cannot the church be hidden." We reply: (1) According to the Hebrew text, the words are like this: "(God) has set its seat for the sun in them," namely in the heavens. The *sensus literalis* [=the intended sense] is that God pitched a tent for the sun, that is, a splendid seat in the heavens. (2) The allegorical interpretation of Augustine, which Bellarmine cites, is drawn from the corrupt Greek and Latin version.

III. They object: "The church or the kingdom of Christ is compared to a mountain, Isa. 2:2; Mic. 4:1–2; Dan. 2:35; in Mat. 5:14 to a city built on a hill that cannot be hid." We reply: (1) Isaiah and Micah prophesy of the call of the Gentiles and their gathering to the church, which is compared in the passage cited to a conspicuous and high hill both [1] because of the ministry of the apostles, which was bound to become famous and to become known everywhere in the world by miracles and wonders, and [2] because of strength and stability. (2) And Daniel means nothing else by this comparison than that, with all the kingdoms of the world destroyed, the kingdom of Christ alone [is] unchanged and will last forever. (3) The passage in Mat. 5:14 does nothing for the perpetual visibility of the church, since Christ does not set forth the distinction and condition of the church under the threefold likeness of light, a city on a hill, and a candle on a candlestick, but reminds His apostles (for the Savior speaks to them, for [this] precedes in verse 13: "You are the salt of the earth," etc.) of their office, lest they hide, or lest they think they can hide themselves and their works, since they are altogether open and are either for example or offense, since both their doctrine and their life would be open to the eyes of all. Therefore the argument drawn from these passages is beside the point. (4) Often also hills and cities built on hills are so engulfed in dense clouds that they can hardly be seen. (5) Just as τὸ ἐξώτερον [the exterior] of a hill is indeed seen with the eyes, but τὸ ἐσώτερον [the interior] is not visible, so indeed does the outward fellowship, administration, and ministry of the church strike the senses, but who are truly inwardly members of the church is not determined by the eyes.

IV. Observe: The Gospel parables of the threshing floor, the net, etc. speak of the outward fellowship of particular churches; we do not deny that this is visible, and there is no other meaning of those parables.

V. Bellarmine objects: "In the Old Testament, those who belonged to the church carried in [their] very flesh a visible sign, namely circumcision; in the New Testament, in the early church, the Holy Spirit was visibly poured out, and those who were added to the church were joined by an outward and visible sign, namely Baptism. Therefore the church was always visible." We reply: [1] Paul in Rom. 2:28-29 distinguishes between a Jew inwardly and outwardly; likewise between circumcision of the flesh and of the spirit. In [Rom.] 9:6 he denies that all are Israelites who are of Israel. Not those who were Jews outwardly, but those who [were Jews] inwardly were true and genuine members of the Israelite church, whose mark was the circumcision that consists in [circumcision] in the spirit, not the letter, and whose praise is not of human beings but of God, Rom. 2 and 9. (2) Outward baptism can be common to the pious and to hypocrites, and therefore certain and infallible judgment regarding members of the catholic church cannot be drawn from it. (3) The miraculous outpouring of the Holy Spirit on the apostles did not make them to be of the church but equipped [them] with extraordinary and necessary gifts for teaching and spreading the Gospel everywhere. (4) And there were particular churches, about which [see] Acts 1:3-4.

VI. [He] objects: "There is no society unless those who are called members recognize it. Now, human beings cannot recognize it unless the bonds of the society are outward and visible. And the church is a society not of angels or of souls but of human beings. Ergo." We reply: [1] There is a union and a society between the church triumphant and [the church] militant (for according to Bellarmine, the church triumphant is united, in fact rather one with [the church] militant), yet it does not rest on outward and visible signs. (2) The souls of dead saints cannot be excluded from the communion of saints. (3) Insofar as one belongs to the outward assembly of some particular church, to that extent he also uses the visible signs of that church; but insofar as he belongs to the catholic church, to that extent he is joined by spiritual bonds, namely faith and love, both with the Head, which is Christ, and with other pious. (4) If there is no fellowship except among those associates who can mutually recognize each other by outward and visible signs, [then] absolutely all fellowship between Christ and the catholic church and its members is denied, since Christ is not seen with the body in this life.

VII. [He] objects: "Those who belonged to the church at the time of Christ shared with the priests by sacrifices in the temple." We reply: Not all who so shared belonged to the true church. In the Jewish church there were high priests, priests, Levites, [and] Pharisees, who all claimed the name of the church for themselves but in fact were not members of the catholic church but enemies and persecutors of Christ and of the true church. And therefore that outward communication is not a sure and infallible sign and indication of the true church.

VIII. Bellarmine objects: "We are all held, under pain of eternal death, to join ourselves to the true church and to persevere in it; but this cannot be done if the church is invisible." We reply: (1) Connection with the outward fellowship of the visible church is not flat-out and absolutely necessary. For inner connection with the universal church is enough unto salvation for a Christian who is held captive in Turkey or [some other] foreign country and cannot join himself to a particular church. (2) And what shall we say about the seven thousand who did not bow their knee to Baal and therefore did not associate themselves with the corrupt church of that time? (3) But we do not deny that every believer and Christian should join himself also to a particular church, provided it exists and is available. (4) One must distinguish between two ways of entering the church. The first is local and clear, to a particular church, by outward profession of faith; the second is spiritual and hidden, to the universal church, by inner assent of the heart. Even though the former may not find a place in time of persecution and of overwhelming corruptions, yet the latter always has a place in the church.

IX. One must distinguish between [1] the people themselves who are gathered as well as the preaching of the Word and the administration of the Sacraments and [2] the faith and election of the people who rightly believe and profitably use the Sacraments. With regard to the former the church is called visible; but with regard to the latter, namely the inner and essential form, which is spiritual fellowship, it is called invisible. For spiritual fellowship, faith, and election are in themselves not evident to human eyes but known to God alone.

X. One must distinguish between [1] members of the church, or people considered materially, namely as they are people and to that extent are visible, and [2] seen formally or insofar as they are members of the true church, or in respect to faith, and to that extent are invisible.

XI. One must distinguish between [1] visible as to the whole and all its parts taken together, and in that way the church universal is invisible both because its intrinsic and essential form cannot be seen and because the individual members, though all are visible, yet they are at such great distance and in so many places that they cannot be observed and penetrated by the eyes, and [2] visible as to the members taken individually and the parts of the members.

XII. One must distinguish between [1] indistinct knowledge, by which I know that, because of the promise of Christ, Luk. 8:8, there always are some in the visible assembly of the called, among whom the seed of the divine Word bears fruit, and [2] distinct and infallible knowledge, [and] since this is not only difficult but also all but impossible in this life, the church itself is therefore called invisible.

XIII. One must distinguish between a particular [church] and the universal, or catholic, church. Though the splendor of a particular church is often very great, yet the catholic church of the saints is invisible.

XIV. One must distinguish between an apodictic [argument] and a probable argument. Recognition of faith from outward works is not apodictic and sure, but only conjectural; error can often underlie it.

Notes:

[1] *Distingu. inter varias vocabuli significationes & acceptiones, quae continent distinctionem aequivoci in sua aequivocata.*

Question III

I. Can the whole catholic and invisible church (or one and all of the believers and the elect) together and at once err and go astray in the fundamental articles of faith, indeed not finally but temporarily?
II. [Can] the visible church sometimes so err in faith and morals that it goes completely astray?

The Point at Issue

The question is not (I) about some particular church but about the universal church. Nor (II) whether the church is absolutely unerring; for we grant that it should properly govern itself in harmony with the order prescribed by God and adhere to the divine Word. Nor (III) [is the question] about the assembly of the infants who die blessedly after Baptism, but about the assembly of the adults who actually exist. Nor (IV) about the assembly of the adults who believe for a time. But (V) about the invisible church of the elect who persevere to the end—whether they can together and at once err and temporarily go astray in the foundation of faith; likewise whether the visible church can sometimes so err in faith and morals that it goes completely astray. Thus Bellarmine himself formulates the point of the question regarding the visible church; he himself embraces the negative part [and] ascribes the positive part to us.

Note: Others formulate the point at issue thus, namely: The question is not about complete defectibility with regard to all articles as well as with regard to all individual [parts], but about defectibility with regard to the outward ministry, so that there would be no conspicuous and visible assembly in the world in which the Word of God would be taught incorruptly; and in this sense the question is whether the church, insofar as it is called a visible universal assembly, can err and go astray, so that the ministry is everywhere corrupted in those [things] and itself does not appear except corrupt, and that middle ground is to be held between [1] the extreme of the papists, who embrace the negative [part], and [2] of the Arminians, who extend the affirmative [part] too broadly and hold that the church can err not only with regard to the outward ministry but also with regard to [its] very essence and existence.

Thesis

The catholic and invisible church, which was from the beginning of the world and is to endure to the end of the world, has together and at once not erred in the foundation of faith, nor does it err, nor can it go astray or be destroyed; but any particular church, though it be planted by Peter, can err, also in fundamentals, in fact go astray not only temporarily but also unto the end, since none of them, and thus also not the Roman [church], has received the prerogative ἀναμαρτησίας [of inerrancy].

Exposition

I. One must distinguish between [1] the universal or catholic church, so called in the absolute sense, or that which embraces all particular [churches] of all places, times, and nations; and this [church] has received from Christ the Head and Bridegroom this prerogative, that the portals of hell will not prevail against it; and [2] any particular church whatever, to which this promise of perpetual existence, duration, and immunity is not given.

II. One must distinguish between [1] total lack of the church, where absolutely no believers are left, or at least so few that they cannot make a church, and [2] a lack with regard to outward splendor, so that they do not constitute any evident assembly visible to all. When one asks if any error can ever so increase that there is not even any public assembly, evident and known to many, that is not infected by that error, our theologians defend the affirmative view, the papists the negative. That is, we hold that absolutely all particular churches, and the whole visible church, can be obscured by a cloud of corruption, errors, heresies, vices, persecutions, etc., and be reduced to the state in which it loses its outward splendor and glory and no evident assembly visible to all or many in the world remains, which [assembly] rejoices in the pure ministry of the Word publicly proclaimed, yet meanwhile there always remain some who hold on to the foundation of faith and preserve faith, hope, and love.

III. One must distinguish between [1] fundamental errors, which overturn the very foundation of faith, and [2] nonfundamental [errors], which can coexist with the foundation of faith [and] meanwhile cling to some questions about faith. The catholic church is subject not to the former but to the latter.

IV. One must distinguish between [1] a particular church considered in the absolute sense and as such and thus immunity from error does not belong to it, and [2] considered respectively or insofar as it continues to be a true and living member of the catholic church and thus cannot err.

V. One must distinguish between [1] the catholic church, which includes the triumphant and the militant church, and [2] the church situated on earth and in conflict with the devil, the world, and the flesh, under the banners of Christ, and the discussion undertaken concerns the latter.

VI. One must distinguish between [1] the universality of bishops and teachers, consisting of whatever number and however much holiness and doctrine, and [2] the universality of all believers. Christ gave this prerogative and this promise, that they cannot err, not to the former but to the latter.

VII. One must distinguish between [1] errors in life, morals, and outward conduct and [2] errors in the doctrine of faith. Also the apostles themselves were subject not to the latter but to the former; see Gal. 2.

VIII. One must distinguish between [1] temporary error, also about fundamental articles, which [error] can be attributed to the elect for a time, yet in such a way that they again escape from it before the end of life, and [2] final [error], in which some particular churches may persevere.

IX. One must distinguish between [1] absolute infallibility, in that one absolutely and positively cannot err, which prerogative belongs only to God and to people led by the Holy Spirit or θεοπνεύστοις [inspired by God], and [2] conditioned [infallibility], insofar as it is the true church and so long as it follows the guidance of the Holy Spirit and hears and embraces only the voice of the Shepherd and Bridegroom.

X. One must distinguish between the Roman church [1] insofar as it denotes the church of the city of Rome and [2] insofar as it denotes other particular churches subject to the Roman pontiff. The apostle expressly teaches, Rom. 11:22, that the former can go astray, and the history of the preceding century abundantly shows that very many of the latter have defected from the Roman pontiff.

XI. The question is not whether the church in an absolute sense cannot fall away, but whether the catholic and invisible church [can fall away]. Bellarmine admits that, saying: "It should be noted that many on our side spend time proving that the church in an absolute sense cannot fall away, for Calvin and the rest of the heretics grant that, but they say it must be understood of the invisible church."

XII. We deny that the church of the New Testament is so bound to some certain see that it is to endure in visible splendor in that certain perpetual succession, like the papists say about the Roman church that that is the sole catholic church in which the pope, the vicar of Christ and successor of Peter, is, in which alone, by perpetual and uninterrupted succession of popes down to present times the truth of the heavenly doctrine has been preserved without any corruption, [and] which had and forever will have outward splendor, so that it can always be seen by all in the whole world.

XIII. Hülsemann rightly [says]: "The papists confess and experience teaches that individual churches planted by the apostles themselves in Jerusalem, Corinth, Galatia, etc. in very fact have fallen away, with the rest of the homogeneous parts or assemblies of the catholic church, both [1] from the fellowship of the influx of faith and of holiness from Christ the Head and [2] from fellowship in line with these qualities. Therefore, when the church is called indefectible from faith and [from] holiness of morals, the whole is understood, homogeneous and gathered out of all particular churches throughout the whole world; and it is pure nonsense and begging the question whatever the papists vaunt and thoughtlessly posit regarding the prerogative and exemption of the Roman church alone from indefectibility."

Antithesis

I. Of the Socinians, who hold that it is not necessary that the church endure perpetually and that the church can go astray completely. Ostorodt says: "The view in which it is held that the church of Christ must always continue and never cease is too presumptuous. Völkel teaches the same. Socinus writes: "I do not deny that there was a full defection under the Antichrist."

II. Of the Arminians, who here follow in Socinian footsteps, teaching that the catholic church can perish and fall away completely. Episcopius says: "We add that it necessarily follows from this (namely that any church can go astray) that the whole and universal church in the world can go astray." And: "And we do not believe that it is necessary for this, [namely] that Christ remain King and Head, that there always be some true church on earth."

III. Of the papists, who say (a) that the church positively and absolutely cannot err in things necessary for salvation nor in other things that it sets before us to believe and do, whether or not they are expressly found in Scripture. Thus Bellarmine says: "The heretics teach that the visible church at times so errs in faith and morals that it goes completely astray; we say the contrary." The same is taught by Stapleton, Becanus, Gordonus, [and] Bailius. (b) That a particular church, and that [church] their own Roman [church], cannot err in faith. Here they mean both the representative church, that is, the prelates and bishops gathered in council, and the virtual [church], that is, the Roman pope.

Confirmation of the Thesis

A. That the whole universal and invisible church can never err or go astray in the fundamental articles of faith is proved (I) from the promises by which perpetual preservation and Christ's presence with it [i.e., the church] are ascribed to the catholic church, Mat. 16:18 and 28:20; Isa. 59:21; Jer. 33:15 and following. Hülsemann well [says]: "That this whole church never departs, has [never] departed, or [never] can depart from the norm of the divine Word either in faith or in deed, both because of the truth of the divine promises and because of the reliability of Him who declared Himself a member of the church, is categorically to be established from Isa. 54:10; Mat. 16:18." And on the passage in Mat. 16:18, "The gates of hell will not prevail against it," observe (1) In these words is promised the firmness and perpetuity of the church, not immutable and perpetual visibility or splendor, such as the papists imagine. For the church can be firm and perpetual, because it is founded on the Rock, though in this world its condition may vary from time to time and its face not always appear the same. (2) By "portals of hell" here is designated the kingdom, might, power, and tyranny of the devil, or the vices, heresies, [and] persecutions that are stirred up and aroused against the church by Satan, the prince of the inhabitants of the infernal regions, and thus it is indicated that no infernal might and power will prevail against the church of Christ and overcome it, but that it stands invincible on Christ, the Rock, to be preserved in steadfastness of the saving truth under the gracious presence of God unto the end of the world. Now, the Savior speaks of the universal church, for the portals of hell often prevail against particular churches, as experience shows. And though it is clear from Christ's point and by reason of the phraseology that the point here is the duration and stability of the church, yet one cannot validly argue from the nonprevalence of the gates of hell to the inerrancy of the universal church with regard to both deadly and final error. Hülsemann says among other things: "It does not follow from the promise of insuperability that the universal church is also free from all danger of erring for a time or [from] temporary error. For this follows neither from the language nor from the purpose of Christ.—It is well known from Luke 24:21 that the faith of Peter and of the rest of the apostles failed for a time." And: "The statement in Mat. 16 is to be taken comparatively, not with regard to all time—so that also the universal church could at no point of time doubt or vacillate regarding any theological truth—but comparatively, with regard to long-lasting teaching of falsehood," etc.

II. From the special providence of God, which promised that it would see to it that the like-minded whole or the universal whole would not go astray or fall away from the truth of the fundamental doctrines and those that are necessary to be believed to obtain salvation, nor also from holiness of morals, according to natural honesty and the Moral Law. (If one asks about sins against conscience or committed deliberately, whether the church can be called impeccable with regard to them, Hunnius replies: "It is certain that such promises are found in Scripture as promise the church of God not only preservation against errors in doctrine but also against the seductions of this world, sins and offenses in conduct, morals and life." Hülsemann also says this.)

III. From the Apostles' Creed: "I believe in the holy catholic church." We confess this also in Art. VII of the Augsburg Confession, namely that there always is and ought to remain the true church. "And this article" (the words are [those] of the Apology, VII-VIII, 9) "is set forth for a necessary reason. ... in order that we may know that though the multitude of the wicked is great, yet the church exists," etc. But suppose that the invisible catholic church can err in fundamental articles of faith and go astray, [then] both our profession of faith will be false (for we believe that that is which is not) and the true church will not last always and forever.

IV. From the absurdities that follow from the opposite view. For in that case Christ would be without a kingdom (on this earth), a head without members, a bridegroom without a bride, a foundation without a superstructure.

Gerhard rightly says: "The whole catholic church never errs in such a way that some do not remain who, following the simple guidance of the Word, under the direction of the Holy Spirit, are sanctified and preserved in the truth and in faith, so that, with the foundation of salvation retained, they are kept by the power of God through faith unto salvation, though they are sometimes few and lie hidden in the most troubled times of the church, so that they are publicly not recognized in the eyes of the world." Dannhauer [says]: "The invisible church is indefectible by universal indefectibility, with regard to τὸ σύνολογον [the whole]; individual believers can fall away; not so the whole church, that is, by divine promises it cannot fail to be that there always is in the world some true church; Christ the king is never without a kingdom."

B. That all particular churches can err is proved (I) from the prophecies or predictions regarding a certain great ἀποστασία [apostasy] and seduction, Mat. 24:24; 1 Tim. 4:1; [and] especially 2 The. 2:3: "The day of the Lord will not come unless there first come ἡ ἀποστασία [the apostasy], defection, and the man of sin be revealed" etc., where, however, the apostle prophesies not about a universal apostasy, *welche die gantze Kirche auf einmal allenthalben überschwemmen and ersäufen werde* [that will swamp and drown the whole church all at once everywhere], but with regard to certain points in time and differences of places and persons." Gerhard rightly [says]: "The apostle clearly speaks of a certain great and nearly universal apostasy, for long ago already the particular [churches] numbered very many."

II. From the threats and warnings, lest they err or be deceived, Mat. 7:15: "Beware of false prophets"; Mat. 24:23-24; Acts 20:28-30; 2 Cor. 11:2-3: "I have joined you to one husband, that I might present you a chaste virgin to Christ," etc. "But I fear, lest, as the serpent deceived Eve with his cunning, so your minds be misled from the simplicity that was over against Christ." Observe (1) The apostle here presents himself as a paranymph or best man. For he says that he ἁρμόζειν [joins], connects, betroths, joins in marriage to Christ all whom he converts to Christianity. This spiritual betrothal namely takes place through faith, by which the bridegroom is received, John 1:12, and lives in the heart of the bride, Eph. 3:17, and it [the heart of the bride] has boldness to approach the bridegroom, Rom. 5:12; Heb. 10:19[-22], but not because of preceding love, as Cornelius a Lapide holds on this passage; for love is a quality of the betrothed spouse but not a means of the mystical betrothal. Observe (2) False teachers laid snares for the virgin brought to Christ only in the simplicity of faith; hence St. Paul feared a shameful apostasy from Christ, and he clarifies it by a comparison with the first Paradisiacal deception. And the sad sequel showed that this fear of the apostles was not idle. For the Corinthian church went astray, so shamefully deflowered by false prophets that we hardly need other than this apostolic proof to show that the true visible church can go astray from Christ, its bridegroom. For why could not what happened to one also happen to another? If the papists object that the nature of the Roman church is other than [that] of the other churches, we ask for sure proofs from Scripture of this difference and special distinction; so far they have not been able to bring it; in fact, the contrary is clear from Rom. 11:21-22 and 16:17, where the apostle threatened the Roman church itself with final destruction. *Die Schlange, die ins Paradies gekrochen, kann auch auf den Römischen Stuhl kommen* [The serpent that crept into Paradise can also get onto the Roman see].

III. From the examples of the particular churches of the Old and New Testaments, namely that they often, and even most [of them], went astray, in fact fell away completely, in fundamental articles of faith; see 1 Cor. 15:12; Gal. 1:6; 4:9. The Israelite church at the time of Moses, under the leadership of Aaron, worshiped an idol, Ex. 32:4. The apostles themselves went astray, following the common error regarding an earthly kingdom of the Messiah and regarding a return of Elijah the Tishbite.

Vindication

As to the passage in Mat. 16:18, "The gates of hell will not prevail," etc., the new Photinians and even Ostorodt and Socinus object (1) that in Scripture *infernum* never means the devil (Arminians have also adopted this [view].) (2) That *infernum* designates the state of the dead, and that the meaning is that those who are Christ's cannot be detained forever in the state of the dead. The Arminians say: "This passage does not promise that the church will always continue to be the church, but only that the church, insofar as it is the church, will never be overcome by death and condemnation." We reply: (1) πύλαι ᾅδου [gates of hell] here mean the infernal strength, judgment, and tyranny of the devil, that is, the vices, heresies, [and] persecutions that Satan stirs up against the church. Here the discussion is not about the word ᾅδης [hell], but what πύλαι ᾅδου [gates of hell] are; and surely that the word ᾅδης [hell], or *inferni* [hell] by metonymy means also the devil in the Scriptures, as in Job 26:6; Pro. 30:16 [KJV: grave]; Rev. 1:18, is well known; and so πύλαι ᾅδου [gates of hell] will be nothing else than the designs and contrivances of the servants of Satan (for decisions and deliberations took place of old at city gates) or the very power of the devil, in order to indicate that the church cannot be overthrown either by the wicked deceptions of heretics or by the manifest power of tyrants. (3) Though, as quite often elsewhere, *infernus* [hell] in this passage be taken of the ποῦ [where] of the devils and the damned, yet that meaning would be that hell with all its power and all forces, and therefore the devils themselves, cannot prevail against the church as it rests on Christ as the altogether sure rock. (4) That simply the state of the dead is somewhere meant by the Greek word ᾅδης [Hades] has not yet been proved, nor is the discussion here about detention in some place but about the power and might that will absolutely not prevail against the church. (5) It is not only the believers who will not remain in the state of death, since also the wicked are to be raised from the dead and so are not to remain in the state of the dead.

As to the passage in Mat. 28:20, "I am with you even to the end of the world," the Socinians, and especially Theophilus Nicolaides, object: "It is not promised that there will always be believers in Christ, but if there always are believers, Christ would also always be with them." We reply: The promise is categorical, not hypothetical. For Christ promises that by His gracious presence and help even unto the end of the world He would gather, preserve, and govern the church on this earth, for which purpose He instituted the ministry of the Word and promised it His παράστασις [presence], lest the work of ministers ever be in vain. "I will be with you even to the end of the world" is not the same as: I will be with you, if you will be with Me, to the end of the world. The Remonstrants, or Arminians, say likewise: "No promise is given to the church in this passage, but only to the founders of the church and to as many ministers as were to follow them in the advancement of evangelical truth; nor is it promised that they will always be and remain or that the church, founded and spread by them, will always remain, but only that Christ will always be with them even to the end of the world." We reply: If Christ will always be with the ministers of the Word, the apostles, in the advancement of evangelical truth, even to the end of the world, what is more certain than that the church itself will remain even to the end of the world? For these, the ministers of the church and the church itself, are related and mutually establish and support each other.[1]

As to the passage in 2 The. 2:3, the papists, especially Bellarmine, object: "By ἀποστασίαν [apostasy] is meant defection from the Roman empire, or complete desolation and overthrow of the Roman empire," and he adds that the Greek and

Latin fathers explain [it] thus. Cornelius a Lapide, with Anselm, Thomas Aquinas, and Estius, also by "defection" understand ἀποστασίαν [apostasy] from the Roman empire or defection from the Roman pontiff and the Roman Catholic Church. We reply: That in this passage is meant defection and withdrawal from the catholic faith, as Lyra explains [it] on this passage, or from the truth and the sincerity of the faith to errors and falsehoods, is pointed out by (a) the point of the apostle, which is, to speak of the sign of the great Antichrist not only [as] significative but causal, namely such a sinful fall [that] from it as from a cause and root, that fruit was to be born—such a fall [that] it provoked divine punishment as a result of thrusting so great a plague on the earth. But now, apostasy from the Roman empire has no causal subordination to the Antichrist. In fact, the papists have scarcely pointed out the word ἀποστασίας [apostasy] used in the New Testament of defection from an earthly realm. Estius writes on this passage: "Defection from an earthly empire can also occur without sin." But apostasy in this passage pertains to that sin and perdition from which the Antichrist is here named. Much less does apostasy from the Roman pontiff and a corrupt church (to fall away from which is to go to God) imply such a causal ranking as apostasy from the faith or, as the apostle says, rejection of the truth [and] faith placed in a lie generates, as Dannhauer rightly teaches. (b) The explanation of Paul himself, 1 Tim. 4:1, where he says: "In the last times ἀποστήσονταί τινες τῆς πίστεως, some will depart from the faith, giving heed to deceitful spirits and doctrines of devils; cf. Acts 20:29–30. (c) The context itself: If the apostle speaks in this passage of apostasy from the Roman empire, he says the same thing twice, for removal of the Roman empire is spoken of in the following verse 7, where another sign of the last day that would precede the revelation of the Antichrist is indicated, namely removal κατέχοντος [of that which restrains]; now, that which restrains is the majesty, terror, [and] violence of the old heathen Roman empire [and] κατέχοντες [those who restrain] were the heathen emperors. Therefore the apostle says: The antichristian majesty of the Roman empire will be removed, namely he that will sit in the church and rule [and] all power, and so also Caesar, will be subject to him. (d) The opinions of the adversaries themselves, which Gerhard gathered and cited. Furthermore, the apostle speaks of a future apostasy through the Antichrist; but now, the Antichrist was to oppose faith and religion, but not the state; therefore this prediction must be understood of ἀποστασία [apostasy] from faith. The apostle adds in the same place: The mystery of iniquity is at work now. However, the Roman empire at the time of the apostles had in no way weakened, but still flourished for a long time.

As to the example of the Israelite church at the time of Moses, Bellarmine objects: "At that time neither the head nor the body of the church went astray. For," he says, "Moses alone was the head (it is certain that he did not err), since Aaron was not yet a priest, for he was made [priest] later, as is clear from Exo. 40:13. The body also did not go astray, for all the Levites were innocent of that sin, as is clear from the same Exo. 32:26, where Moses says, 'If anyone be [on] the Lord's [side], let him join with me,' and all the sons of Levi rallied to him." Becanus repeats the same. We reply: (1) This passage clearly shows that the church can fail only in what is set forth, yet be invisible. For the people of Israel as a whole then engaged in idolatry, nor, on the other hand, was there any group incorrupt and visible in which the sincere and pure worship of God flourished publicly. And though there were some among the Israelites whom that idolatry displeased, for the apostle says, 1 Cor. 10:7, that τίνες, some, of the Israelites were idolaters, yet they were hidden and did not constitute any visible group. (2) Moses was ruler and mediator of the people, however not high priest, but this honor was conferred by divine command on Aaron. (3) And at that time Moses lingered on the mount and appointed Aaron and Hur in his place; the people should obey them. Therefore not Moses but Aaron and Hur were the heads of the visible church; from this it is clear that, with Aaron instituting idolatrous worship of a male calf, the head itself erred and went astray. (4) We grant that some among the people were not contaminated by this idolatry, but in comparison with the rest they were few, who could not hinder that idolatry. Hence it is said in a general way that the people demanded molten gods, verse 1, that the people offered earrings, verse 3, [and] that God was angry with the people and wanted to destroy them all, verse 10; nor is it very likely that absolutely none of the Levites consented to this μοιχολατρείαν [adulterous worship], since the head of this family was Aaron, whose example and guidance many doubtless followed; but that later, verse 26, they rallied to Moses and inflicted punishment on the rebellious—this shows that, led by true repentance, they returned to a sounder mind.

Refutation of Objections

I. Observe: The predicate, or indefectibility (or inability to fall away from faith and holiness), is not to be taken categorically, like "God cannot lie [and] cannot die," but (1) hypothetically, in relation to the divine promise and providence, which promised that He would see to it that not the whole homogeneous body would go astray (for the promise of indefectibility was made to the whole homogeneous body of the church, not to these or those particular groups). (2) It is to be taken in a comparative way, in relation to the main objects of perseverance, or the fundamental articles of faith and morals; (3) in a comparative way, not with regard to moments of time, that also the whole church could at no point in time doubt regarding any theological truth or vacillate, but in a comparative way, with regard to long-lasting teaching of falsehood, that the universal church could teach no theological falsehood, because of the constant assistance of the Holy Spirit, yet in such a way that just as the presence of the living Spirit does not prevent failures of courage,[2] so the constant assistance of the Holy Spirit does not keep the teaching[3] of the church from vacillating sometimes at the time when there is danger that the elect be misled. (4) With regard to degree of both knowledge and faith as well as of holiness and morals, we firmly hold together with the Romans, that the collective universal church, embracing each and every teacher and hearer, simply cannot fall away from the truth of doctrines [that are] fundamental and necessary to be believed to obtain salvation, nor also from holiness of morals according to natural uprightness and the Moral Law in such a way that as a valid consequence murders, adulteries, thefts, and other similar crimes would ever be approved by all the faithful or be put into practice itself.

II. Observe: The church is called holy because it is called with a holy calling, because it is gathered under a holy Head, Christ, because it shares in His holiness, because it is sanctified by Christ through the Holy Spirit, because it pursues holiness [and] because it aims for perfect holiness in the life to come, not because it lacks all blemish both in life and in morals. But now if this holiness does not keep the church from having its blemishes in life, it will also not keep it from having blemishes in doctrine.

III. One must distinguish between the whole church[4] and the whole of the church.[5] The whole church can err, fall, and go astray, but not all of the church in the divided sense. When the Savior says, Mat. 16:18, "The gates of hell will not prevail against it," He speaks of the whole of the church and the invisible church, which God preserves for Himself in grace in the visible church even unto the end, John 14:16; 16:12.

IV. One who says that the invisible church cannot err once and together does not make of the church an unerring numen or one equal to God, because identity of gift does not suffice for equality, but there is required in addition the same manner of having [it]. Angels and souls of people are also immortal, by grace, yet they are not therefore equal to God. So also is the church not made equal to God by reason of the distinction of inerrability, for God is such of Himself and His nature, [but] the church is [such] by the grace and promise of God.

V. They object: "It is absurd to say that the bride of Christ can become a harlot, for in that way Christ Himself and the Holy Spirit would be pierced through the side of the bride." We reply: That elect assembly of the justified is and remains the bride of Christ. We do not hesitate to say that the visible church can turn from a faithful spouse into a harlot, yet preserved by the Son of God [as] His bride. The visible church, I say, can be a harlot, yet under her lie hidden the bride of the Son of God, namely that assembly which embraces His doctrine and perseveres in true faith.

VI. Bellarmine objects: "In 1 Tim. 3:15 the church is called the pillar and ground of the truth." We reply: (1) There are some who would not have that "pillar and ground of the truth" to be connected with the word "church" but join it to what follows, so that what the apostles calls "without controversy the great mystery of godliness" is that "pillar and ground of the truth," that is, the chief article of faith and of religion. (2) One must distinguish between ground and foundation; likewise between [1] ground in the absolute sense and [2] μετά τι [relatively], or so called with certain limitations. A particular church is a ground of truth, not a foundation, not a ground in the absolute sense, but μετά τι [relatively]or with a certain limitation, insofar as it rests on heavenly truth, comprehended in Scripture, as on a foundation. It befits a house to have a foundation and pillars, not to be a foundation and a pillar. (3) The church is called ἑδραίωμα [support], *gleichsam ein Bücherschab* [as it were a bookshelf], a stand *darauf die* [on which the] records *der Göttlichen Wahrheit* [of divine truth] are put *und beygeleget* [and kept]. (4) One must distinguish between a pillar of the truth in an architechtonic sense and a pillar of the truth in a political sense. The church is a pillar of the truth not in an architechtonic sense, in such a way that it strengthens and supports the truth, like a pillar supports a building, but in a political sense, insofar as it holds the tables of the divine law affixed and bears the Gospel as it were inscribed and displays [it] like a pillar, just as the decrees of the supreme magistrate were usually attached to pillars of palaces and were suspended from them. In an architechtonic sense, the church is not a pillar of Scripture, but Scripture is the pillar, foundation, and ground of the church and of faith, as the apostle teaches, Eph. 2:20. (5) If the church at Ephesus, of which the apostle here speaks in particular and obviously, were in an absolute sense and without reservation the pillar and ground of the truth, it would have remained free of error; but the opposite of this is clear from Acts 20 and Rev. 2 as well as from historical accounts.

VII. They object: "The church is always ruled by Christ as Head, Eph. 1:22-23; 4:15; [and] 5:23; and therefore it is put beyond danger of going astray as one that is led by the Spirit of Christ into all truth, John 16:13." We reply: (1) If the church is always ruled by Christ as the Head, there is no need for the pope as vicar. (2) As long as and inasfar as the church is ruled by Christ as Head, so long and insofar it rests beyond all danger of error, according to the statements of Isa. 59:21; John 8:31; 14:26; 16:13-14; etc. (3) In John 16:13, "The Holy Spirit will lead you into all truth," Christ speaks πρώτως [primarily] and principally of the apostles and of the truth that one must absolutely know. But the promises made to the church regarding the instruction of the Holy Spirit and the direction and indwelling of God are conditional, Jer. 7:3; John 8:31; 15:7.

VIII. They object: "Believers are obligated, under pain of anathemas, to believe the church in all things, as is clear from Mat. 18:17: 'If he will not hear the church,' etc. All councils pronounce anathemas on those that do not agree with the decrees of the church." We reply: The church is to be heard, but the true [church] and the one that hears Christ. Now, this one is built on the foundation of the prophets and apostles, Eph. 2:20. But if the church degenerates and teaches things other than the prophetic and apostolic doctrine, it is not to be heard, as Christ says, Mat. 16:11-12; John 10:27; Mat. 28:19; and [as] Paul [says] Gal. 1:8; and John, 2 John 5. (2) If the passage of Matthew would mean infallibility in doctrine, [then] also any particular church would be free from the suspicion of error. (3) But it does not speak of infallibility in doctrine, but especially of brotherly admonition and ecclesiastical censures. (4) And the anathemas of the councils bind in no other way than as they are pronounced on those who stir up opposition against manifest truth in the Scriptures. (5) It does not follow: The church should be heard as it exhorts transgressors of the divine law to repentance; therefore it is not possible that the church can ever err regarding articles of faith and fall away from the true faith.

IX. Bellarmine objects: "If the church could err, the greatest part of the doctrines of faith could be called into question, in fact especially the canon of Scripture." We reply: We believe in the canonical Scriptures not so much because of the testimony of the church as because of their authority, sublimity, efficacy, divine majesty, harmony, and sufficiency, as well as the inner testimony of the Holy Spirit speaking in them.

X. Observe: When Christ promises the Comforter to His disciples, who would remain with them forever, then He speaks of conditioned μονῇ [abiding] and guidance, namely as long as they would adhere to the truth and allow themselves to be led by it.

XI. One must distinguish between [1] the promises of the perpetuity and ἀναμαρτησία [sinlessness] of the church, which are sure and also certainly fulfilled, and [2] the manner and subject of fulfillment. They are always fulfilled, if not in the visible or flourishing church, yet in the church invisible or the hidden sheepfold of the elect.

XII. One must distinguish between [1] absolute promises that God will gather and preserve for Himself a church in mankind and [2] conditioned [promises that He will gather a church], namely in a certain particular church, if the sheep hear the voice of the Great Shepherd.

XIII. In Scripture it is never said of the church that it cannot err, not even for a moment, because it says in a formal way that sinlessness cannot err, which does not fit the church militant by nature, because it is contradictory to say that believers are militant and cannot sin.

XIV. It is not valid to argue from [good] angels to the elect. The [good] angels, both collectively and individually, cannot err; but the elect, though not all at the same time, yet individually can err, temporarily, but not to the end. It is therefore false that our view turns God's admonitions into *Spötterey, wie es Spötterey wäre, wann ich die Engel im Himmel warnen und sagen wolte, hütet euch, ihr Engel, daß euch der Satan nicht verführe,* etc. [mockery, as it would be mockery if I would warn the angels in heaven and say, "Be on your guard, you angels, that Satan may not mislead you," etc.]. For the angels are confirmed in bliss.

XV. It is certain that the elect can err for a time because of the going astray of pseudo-Christians, but not to the end. What follows, εἰ δυνατὸν, "if possible," Mat. 24:24, does not say that also temporary sinlessness and inerrability of the elect is imparted to the church, but indicates a difficulty that the Savior nevertheless overcomes in His extraordinary grace and absolute power.

XVI. Observe: Both are certain: The church is preserved unconquered on the rock (Mat. 16:18) in the assurance of the saving truth under the gracious presence of God even to the end of the world, and yet it is defectible and has actually gone astray, not even the Roman [church] excepted. These things cannot be harmonized with each other except by distinction between [1] the invisible, invincible, unceasing church and [2] the visible, vincible [church] that will end.

Notes:

[1] *se mutuo ponunt et tollunt.*
[2] *animi.*
[3] *sensus.*
[4] *totam ecclesiam.*
[5] *totum ecclesiae.*

Question IV

Are the essential and perpetual marks of the church the pure preaching of the divine Word and the proper[1] use of the Sacraments?

The Point at Issue

I. The question is not about the Christian church in general in contradistinction to sects of the Jews, Turks, pagans, but about the orthodox church in particular, in contradistinction to the rest of the sects of Christians. (II) The question is not about verisimilar, common, and accidental marks and signs, but of infallible, proper, perpetual, and essential signs and marks, from which it can be surely and infallibly concluded that this is the true church. (III) [The question is not] about the church to be established, but about the established church. (IV) [The question is not] about the invisible church but about the visible church.

Thesis

The primary, unquestioned, perpetual, and essential marks of the true church on this earth, by which it can be surely and infallibly both recognized and pointed out to others and be distinguished from any and all other assemblies are two: the pure preaching of the divine Word and the proper administration of the Sacraments.

Exposition

I. One must distinguish between [1] the Christian church in general, as it is contradistinguished from sects of the Jews, Turks, pagans, which is recognized by the profession of Christian doctrine and the Holy Bible,[2] just as the Turkish assembly [is recognized] by the Koran of Mohammed, the Jewish by the Talmud, etc. and [2] the orthodox church in particular, contradistinguished from the other sects of Christians, Calvinists, papists, etc.; the question is not about the former, but about the latter. That is: In this question the discussion is not about distinguishing those who outwardly profess Christianity from the heathen, Jews, or Turks, because the very name "Christian" and the profession of Baptism points them out sufficiently; but [the discussion is] therefore about distinguishing the true and genuine church of Christ among the assemblies of Christians who give themselves the name of the true church. We look for the marks of the true church (1) that are in the church itself, (2) that are very well known by the church, (3) by which the true church of Christ may be distinguished not only from heathen unbelievers, Jews, etc. but also from heretical assemblies, [and] (4) that fit the true church only and always and are proper to it.

II. One must distinguish between [1] infallible, full,[3] perpetual, and essential marks of the orthodox church and [2] verisimilar, common, and accidental marks of the church. The marks of the papalists are in no way proper and infallible or essential to the church, but spurious and fallible, because they simply do not fit the church, as noted, or as accidental to it, or are also common with a false church.

III. Or, one must distinguish between [1] the proper and essential marks of the church that both [a] designate the true, catholic, and apostolic church closely and fully and [b] distinguish [it] from other, heterodox assemblies and [2] common and accidental marks [that are] neither proper nor perpetual and therefore false, as are the name "Catholic," antiquity, large size, miracles, temporary felicity, etc.

IV. One must distinguish between [1] marks of those who definitely believe truly, who then they may be and by what τεκμηρίοις [signs] they might be recognized, and [2] marks of those who indefinitely believe, namely where some communion of believers may be gathered or it may be necessary to seek believers in some assembly. Certainly distinct knowledge of believers does not fall under the view and judgment of human beings. For only God knows His own, 2 Tim. 2:19. But we can recognize the communion of believers itself or the church itself taken collectively. Or, though those who are definitely and personally true and living members of the church cannot be recognized infallibly by marks, yet one must not grant that one cannot know indefinitely and in general where, then, there is an assembly of saints and of true believers. For wherever the Word of God is preached purely and the Sacraments are administered properly and rightly, there is no doubt that some believers are gathered to the catholic communion of saints there, though it may not be possible for any human beings to establish for sure how many and who indeed they are.

V. One must distinguish between [1] that there is some church that falsity can underlie, wherefore its marks can be some kind of preaching of the divine Word and some kind of use of the Sacraments, and [2] the true church, just as it was at other times usually distinguished among disciples of Christ and true believers, John 8:31; the discussion here is not about the former but about the latter.

VI. One must distinguish between the church to be established and [the church that is] established. The former, because it does not yet exist but is at length gathered to God by the Word and the Sacraments, can therefore not be recognized and pointed out by definite marks. But the latter, namely [the church] that is constituted, since it proclaims and commends the Word of God to others and administers the Sacraments, thereby reveals and shows itself to others.

VII. One must distinguish between [1] the invisible church, which is known only to God, who searches the hearts and the reins, and which cannot be infallibly either known or pointed out by us in this life, and [2] the visible church, under which the invisible [church] is contained, which can be recognized by us by certain marks.

VIII. Observe: The question is not whether the proper administration of the Sacraments is a mark of the church at all times, for the church lacked the Sacraments, strictly so called, up to the time of Abraham, but whether, with the use of the now properly instituted Sacraments posited, they also concur and sustain the nature of some mark.

IX. That question regarding the marks of the church is altogether worthy of earnest discussion, because the hinge of salvation turns on this, that we recognize the true church and when it is recognized, join ourselves to it, and after we have joined ourselves to it persevere in it.

Antithesis

I. Of the papists, who deny that pure preaching of the divine Word and the proper use of the Sacraments are perpetual and essential marks of the true church. For example, Bellarmine, Stapleton, Gordon Huntley, Pistorius, [and] others. And on the other hand they set up 15 other marks of the church in the same Bellarmine, namely (1) the name "Catholic"; (2) antiquity; (3) durability or long duration; (4) large size; (5) episcopal succession; (6) harmony in doctrine with the ancient church; (7) unity of members among themselves and with the head; (8) holiness of doctrine; (9) efficacy of the same; (10) holiness of the life of pastors; (11) the glory of miracles (where [there are] miracles, there [is the] church, says Lipsius); (12) prophetic light; (13) the admission of the adversaries; (14) the unhappy end of enemies; and (15) finally, temporal happiness divinely conferred on those who have defended the church. "For," Bellarmine adds, "the Catholic princes have never followed God" (read: the Roman

Antichrist) "wholeheartedly but that they triumphed easily over [their] enemies." Yet these marks do not always belong to the true church, since they are common to other assemblies. Surely the Jesuit did not want to overwhelm us with the number of marks because he could not by weight.

II. Of the Socinians, who likewise deny that profession of pure doctrine and proper use of the Sacraments are true and essential marks of the church. "There are no marks of the church, nor can there be any that deserve to be called that," says Theophilus Nicolaides. Smalcius says: "There is indeed no true and pure doctrine except in the true church, and the true church cannot exist without true, or to speak more correctly, saving doctrine; yet true and saving doctrine is not a mark of the church, but it is the form of the church, namely that which gives it being." Völkel teaches the same, speaking against the marks of the church.

III. Of the Arminians, who in the controversy about the marks of the church seem to approach the camp of the Socinians. For they deny that preaching of the Word is a mark of the church: "Therefore, because preaching is at times an instrument for gathering the church it cannot be a sure and infallible mark of the gathered church." And: "It is, in fact, so, that the Remonstrants do not acknowledge the preaching of the Word and the use of the Sacraments as marks. Yet in the point at issue they are not consistent."

IV. Of the Weigelians, who also with the papists do not accept the pure preaching of the divine Word and the proper use of the Sacraments as essential and perpetual marks but substitute love of the neighbor as the infallible mark of the church.

Confirmation of the Thesis

The thesis is proved (I) by the very definition of the visible church, which is the assembly of human beings who embrace the Word of God and use the Sacraments, John 8:31; 10:27; 14:23; Eph. 5:26.

II. By the requisites of marks properly so called, which are: (1) solely and always to fit the thing that is noted and to distinguish it from others; (2) clearly to point out the thing that is noted. Now, all these things fit the preaching of the Word and the administration of the Sacraments. By this as by a scarlet thread in the Jericho[4] of this world the true house of Rahab, in which alone is salvation, is discerned.

III. By the connection between cause and effect. For every particular effect points to a proximate and adequate cause. Now, to preach the Word and administer the Sacraments is a particular effect of the church or of the ministers, who carry out that office in the name of the church. Ergo.

IV. Our line of reasoning is this: That which is (1) perpetually connected with the true church, (2) never separated from it, (3) fits it alone, (4) meets the senses, and (5) is better known than the church itself,[5] that is a mark of the church. Now, the preaching of the Word and the use of the Sacraments are such. Ergo.

V. What distinguishes the true church from a church of the wicked is a proper mark of the church. The pure preaching of the Word and the proper use of the Sacraments distinguish the true church from the church of the wicked. Ergo. The minor [premise] is proved: For these two (1) of old distinguished the Israelite church in the Old Testament from the heathen, Deu. 4:6; Psa. 147:19–20; Gen. 17:10–11; Exo. 12:48. (2) Pure doctrine distinguishes a true prophet from a false one, Mat. 7:16; Stapleton himself interprets this passage of doctrines. (3) Of old the Arians were distinguished from the orthodox in no other way than by doctrine.

VI. What was a mark of the early church at the time of the apostles, that is also now a mark of the church. Reception of the apostolic doctrine, Baptism, and the breaking of bread were marks of the early church at the time of the apostles, Acts 2:40–42. Therefore reception of the apostolic doctrine, Baptism, and the breaking of bread are also now marks of the church.

VII. By what the church is established, materially and formally, by that it is also marked. The church is established materially and formally by the Word that is preached and by Scripture. Ergo. The minor [premise] is clear from Mat. 28:19: μαθητεύσατε [make disciples of] all nations, baptizing them, teaching them to obey, etc.; 1 Ptr. 1:23; Rom. 10:14; Tit. 3:5; 1 Cor. 4:5. The church is born out of the Gospel and Baptism, and Christ μορφοῦται [is formed] in us by the Gospel, Gal. 4:19. Likewise: The things by which the church is established, fostered, and preserved, that is an infallible sign and mark of the church. Now, by the preaching of the Word and the administration of the Sacraments, etc. Ergo. The connection with the major [premise] is proved, because nothing greater can infallibly mark something than that by which something is established, for this cognition is cognition through the cause and thus infallible and unchangeable. The minor is proved by John 8:31, where Christ says: "If you continue in My Word, you will be My disciples," etc. "My sheep hear My voice, and they follow Me," John 10:27. Therefore the sheep is His in which His voice resounds. The church is engendered by Baptism, Eph. 5:26–27; Tit. 3:5.

Moreover, that the papistic marks are not true, infallible, and perpetual marks of the church is proved by the following:

First, marks need to be better known than the thing that is noted, namely the church. Therefore these are not marks of the church. Second, marks need to be proper and inseparable. The name "Catholic," antiquity, long duration, large size, etc. are not proper to the church and inseparable from it. Ergo.

1. Not the name "Catholic." For (a) it was not always in the church. The name "Christian" was used in the early church, deep silence with regard to "Catholic." (b) The Arians and Donatists attached this name to themselves. (c) Names that are humanly assumed are not ἀποδείκτικα [definitive]. (d) It does not fit the Roman church truly but only ὁμωνύμως [equivocally]. "Mother church is called Catholic," says Augustine, "because it is universally perfect and wavers in nothing and is spread throughout the world." But the Roman church is particular and abounds in heresies.

II. Not antiquity. For (a) this belongs also to the kingdom of Satan and the assembly of the wicked, but not always to the church of Christ, especially when it was very young. (b) What is apart from the truth is of no importance, [says] Cyprian. (c) It does not belong to the Roman church, because the Roman congregation is new in newness of doctrine and rites. (d) Antiquity is not an attribute flowing from its form. For the number of years is outside of the things whose years are counted. Nor is old age truly γνώρισμα [a mark] of the true human being or of good state.

III. Not long duration. For (a) it is common to the Mohammedan sect and to the Jewish synagogue. (b) It is not better known than the church. (c) We call those the marks of the church that are actually in the church, but not those that are very much hoped for or expected in the future.

IV. Not large size or great number. For (a) in the early youth the church did not have temples. (b) Under the Antichrist, Rev. 13:8, and near the end of the world it will not be large, Luke 18:8. Bellarmine for certain has it, that it will come to pass, that at the time of the Antichrist all ceremonies, sacrifices, and exercises of public religion will cease. (c) The assembly[6] of Satan is always larger than the church of Christ. For the latter is a little flock, Luke 12:32, and they are few, who enter by the narrow way of salvation, Mat. 7:14. "How far, pray," writes Sonnius, bishop of Antwerp, "does the Catholic church now extend through the habitable world? Scarcely three ells long in comparison with the vastness that the assembly of Satan possesses." (d) And what religion is larger than the Mohammedan today? (e) And greatness is a mark of the woman in Revelation, Rev. 17:15. "The whole world will follow the beast in wonder and worship it," Rev. 13:3, 8.

V. Not local and official succession of bishops. For (a) succession in doctrine and faith is to be properly regarded as succession, but that succession in the papacy as to apostolic doctrine is corrupt. (b) Local succession is common also to the assembly of the Jews, which condemns Christ, as well as [that] of the Arians and schismatics. (c) It does not belong to the church at all times, for Paul predicts a succession of wolves, Acts 20:29. (d) The church existed before there was a succession of bishops.

(e) A mere succession of persons without a succession of true doctrine is a title without substance and a patroness of fiction. (f) And if heresy breaks the line of succession, the succession of the Roman see, on which so many heretical and wicked popes have sat, ceased long ago. Dannhauer speaks at length of both corruptions and interruptions of the papal office.

VI. Not harmony of doctrine with the ancient church. For (a) heretics also boast that harmony. (b) No one can be certain about that harmony unless he read all the writings of the Greek and Latin fathers; meanwhile you must be sure regarding the church. (c) The church was before the fathers were. (d) The papists want harmony with the fathers to be a mark of the true church and appeal to them as to judges in controversies of faith, so as to deflect the tribunal of Scripture, whose judgment they fear. They are, as Tertullian says, heretics that flee the light of the Scriptures. (e) Why do they not want harmony of doctrine with Holy Scripture to be a mark of the true church? Because the authority[7] of Scripture is far greater and [its] rule[8] more certain and [its] light more manifest.[9]

VII. Not union not only of the members of the church among themselves but also with a head (namely a visible [head]). For (a) there was union also among the prophets of Baal, who conspired against Micaiah, 1 Kin. 22:13, among those who asked that a golden calf be made, Exo. 32:1, those who supported the idolatrous worship of Diana of the Ephesians against Paul, Acts 19:29, [and] those who followed the Antichrist, Rev. 13:16. (b) On the other hand, there can be dissension between true churches, just as there was between the Eastern and Western churches regarding Easter. (c) The Roman congregation itself is divided against itself both by studies of religions, [studies] born out of the very genius of religions, as well as by views also regarding faith, [views] at war among themselves by formal contradiction. For example: The pope is superior to a council; the pope is not superior to a council. Spain, Italy, [and] the whole school of the Jesuits hold the former; all of Gaul and the remaining parts of Europe hold the latter. (d) We hold the necessary union of the church under the one Head, Christ; but union under the one head, the Roman pope, is so very incongruous for us to believe that it is a mark of the church, that we believe, on the contrary, that he is a perforated ulcer and a cancerous ulcer on the body of the Roman church, and one who is united with the Roman pope cannot be united with Christ.

VIII. Not holiness of doctrine. For (a) that holiness cannot be separated from doctrine itself. Therefore they grant that holy doctrine must be a true mark of the church. Holiness of doctrine cannot be recognized when its truth is not known, nor can that be true doctrine, which incites to vices and opposes holiness of morals. Truth of doctrine comes before knowledge of the holiness of the same doctrine. For light of intellect precedes in order uprightness of the will, because the intellect lights the way for[10] the will. Therefore holiness of doctrine cannot be a mark of the church to them who are ignorant of the truth of the doctrine. (b) Holiness of doctrine does not fit the Roman assembly,[11] inasmuch as it is apostate heresy, out of which, as fruit from a tree that as such is bad, flows the scum of sins. (c) Blemishes of which our church is often accused are disapproved by Dannhauer.

IX. Not efficacy of doctrine. For (a) the verdict is the same regarding this. (b) That efficacy is evaluated either out of persuasion alone, or by violent compulsion, or by salutary conversion to God. The last does not fit the Roman church, the first is not proper to true doctrine alone but is common to the doctrine of heretics, which often moves and deceives many. The second is common in the papacy, since it [uses] sanguinary tortures of consciences and well-known inquisitorial syllogisms, in the conclusion of which there enter crosses, swords, flames, wheels, etc.

X. Not holiness of life of the leaders or of the chief teachers of religion. For (a) outward holiness is common also to hypocrites, who have the form of godliness—holiness, I say, in appearance, front, [and] looks, [but] not in the heart. Satan himself transforms himself into an angel of light. [And] inward holiness does not strike the senses. (b) The popes, architects of the papistic hierarchy, were monsters given over to pride, lust, robbery, poisonings, and to every sin of audacity, as the fawning flatterers of the popes, Baronius, Genebrard, Platina, Sigonius, Dietrich von Nieheim, etc. themselves say. But we have Christ and the apostles [as] the authors of our religion, much holier[12] than Gregory VII, John VIII and XXIII,[13] Alexander III and IV, Boniface VIII, and the rest of such monsters. (c) One who is a Jew in secret is truly a Jew, Rom. 2:29. The more hidden holiness is, the more pleasing it is to God, Mat. 6:5.

XI. Not the glory of miracles. For (a) Bellarmine himself confesses: "Before the proof of the church it is not evident or sure with the certainty of faith regarding any miracle that it is a true miracle." When, therefore, the papists make miracles a mark of the church, they beg the question and go in a circle. For they try to prove the truth of the church from the truth of miracles and the latter in turn from the former, which is clearly going in a circle. (b) It is common also to the Egyptian magicians, Exo. 7:11-12; to false prophets, Deu. 13:3; Mat. 7:22; and to the Antichrist, 2 The. 2:9; Rev. 13:13; in fact also to the heathen. (c) In the church of the New Testament it needed to last only for a while, and many ages have passed in which the true church had no miracles. (d) The miracles performed by Christ and the apostles established authority for the Gospel now, even though miracles have ceased. (e) "If you are a believer," says Chrysostom, you do not need signs, for signs are given to unbelievers." In fact, just as someone is more vile, so is he more desirous of miracles, as Christ Himself says, Mat. 12:39: "A wicked and adulterous people seeks signs." (f) Maldonatus, on Mat. 7:22, confesses that false prophets and heretics can perform miracles.

XII. Not prophetic light. For (a) it is not a perpetual gift to the orthodox church but [is] peculiar to the beginnings of the church. (b) It is not valid to argue affirmatively from an event to the θεόπνευστον [divinely inspired] light of prophecy properly so called, though it is valid negatively, Deu. 18:22. (c) Also heathen and false prophets at times either had or claimed [prophetic light], e.g., Balaam, Num. 23; the Sibyls, Apollonius of Tyana, etc. (d) He that foretold the death of Saul on the morrow was a true demon in the role of Samuel.

XIII. Not the admission of the adversaries. For (a) this is neither universal nor perpetual, but accidental and contingent. (b) And it is not better known. (c) Nor do we lack the same admission.

XIV. Nor the unhappy end of those who oppose the church. For (a) many persecutors of the church have died peacefully, like Trajan, Aurelius, Antonius Verus, Septimius Severus, etc. On the other hand, Josiah, a vigorous defender of the church, the apostles, martyrs, and many pious perished miserably. (b) It is not better known, but leaves the mind in doubt.

Nor finally XV. the happiness of defenders of the church. For (a) if this were a mark of the true church, the church of old would rather have been among the Philistines, Assyrians, Persians, and Romans than among the Israelites and Jews. For how often did the Philistines, Ammonites Midianites, Assyrians, Babylonians, Romans, etc. prevail in battle against the Israelites (who, no one doubts, had the true religion). Very often also an expedition against the Turks was undertaken by the papists, but they came out victors scarcely once or twice; for the most part they withdrew in the face of various blows. (b) For the most part the wicked are happier in this world, Jer. 12:1; Psa. 73:3–5 ff. But the pious are subject to afflictions, which examples of nearly all ages show, etc. (c) The Anglo-Rheims [commentators], in notes on Mat. 5, clearly confess: "Prosperous successes of people or of nations are no sign of very true or very pure religion."

Vindication

As to the passage in John 10:27, "My sheep hear My voice," therefore the church is where the Word of God is heard, Bellarmine objects: "This passage in no way teaches where the church is, but who the elect are, namely those who from the heart perseveringly hear and keep the Word; but since it cannot be known who hear from the heart, this cannot be a mark of the visible church." We reply: (1) It indeed cannot be known by us for certain who hear the voice of Christ from the heart and follow Him and are therefore elect; but we can know this, that wherever the voice of Christ is heard, some are there who hear it from the heart, because the voice of Christ has the added efficacy of the Holy Spirit and therefore is not heard without fruit. Now then, wherever some are who hear the voice of Christ, there are the elect, [and] where the elect are, there is the church. (2) Though it cannot be known who from the heart hear the voice of Christ perseveringly, yet we can hear the voice of Christ sounding publicly in the assembly of the church, and we can likewise determine whether the preaching of the Word heard in a public assembly agrees with the voice of Christ set before us in the Holy Scriptures; therefore we can also learn thoroughly from this mark who the true sheep of Christ and the true members of the church are.

As to the passage in Eph. 5:25-27, "Christ loved the church ... cleansing [it] with the washing of water by the Word": The church is cleansed by the Word; therefore wherever the cleansing Word is, there the church is. Bellarmine objects: "That cleansing is invisible, and Paul does not teach there what or where the church is, but what blessing God bestows on the church." We reply: (1) Baptism is a blessing proper to the church; therefore wherever true and pure Baptism is administered, there a church is gathered unto God. (2) It can be firmly concluded on the basis of this apostolic passage that Baptism is a mark of the church, because the apostle binds the church to Baptism and asserts that Baptism is not administered except within the church, saying pointedly: "Christ sanctified the church with the washing of water by the Word."

Bellarmine disregards the stronger foundations of our position.

Refutation of Objections

I. Observe: The preaching of the Gospel and the administration of the Sacraments, in a different way of looking at it, are the formal cause, the effect, and function of the church. They are the formal cause, namely of the church to be established and preserved, and the function and effect of the church [that is] already established, insofar as it teaches and informs others; therefore these marks mark and point out the church both from cause to effect[14] and from effect to cause.[15]

II. One must distinguish between [1] preaching of the Word taken in a general way for profession of doctrine by all members of the church, pastors and hearers in common and for public teaching of Bible passages, which is also a kind of preaching, Acts 15:21, and [2] preaching taken in the narrow sense, which is rather a proper action of a pastor than of the whole church in common; nor is it simply and absolutely necessary for the church, as is shown by times of most grievous persecutions, in which it was possible for the church to be preserved solely by the reading of Scripture, without public preaching or pure doctrine. When the preaching of the Word is specified as a mark of the church, it is taken not in the latter but in the former sense.

III. One must distinguish between [1] purity itself, which can be to some extent also in sectarian assemblies, and [2] degrees of purity, which vary. Accordingly, the purer and truer the doctrine is, the purer and truer the church is, and the less pure the doctrine [is], the less pure and more corrupt the church will be, although because of this impurity it does not immediately cease to be the church.

IV. One must distinguish between [1] purity or impurity of some whole church consisting of pastors and hearers and [2] purity or impurity of some of its members, whether pastors or hearers, whose impurity is not immediately to be charged to the whole church.

V. Observe: There are certain grades of preaching pure doctrine, since the Word of God is preached sometimes more purely, sometimes less purely in the church; and it does not immediately cease to be the church, even if to the greatest degree impure doctrine is taught in some chief parts of religion, because God can beget and preserve a holy seed and spiritual children for Himself also when the public ministry of the visible church is corrupt.

VI. One must distinguish between [1] unbelievers and heathen situated outside the church, to whom, since they recognize neither the Word nor the Sacraments, the authority of Scripture must first be pointed out before they might judge regarding the truth of the church on the basis of doctrine, and [2] heterodox among Christians, who [the heterodox] are vague about the truth of the assembly of Christians and orthodox.

VII. One must distinguish between [1] confused or imperfect knowledge that is drawn from common accidents, separable externals, and adjacent matters, which [knowledge] rests on sole probability, and [2] distinct and perfect knowledge that flows from its own out of the essence of the matter and is demanded by its actions; and this generates sometimes knowledge, sometimes faith.

VIII. One must distinguish between [1] a probable way of pointing out the church, which is drawn from common signs and is manuductory to further investigation, and [2] an apodictic and infallible way of pointing out [the church].

IX. One must distinguish between [1] the natural ability to know the truth, which [ability] is confused, defective, in fact insignificant and useless, [and] therefore neither the heterodox nor the heathen know the church in this way, and [2] the supernatural or divinely infused [ability to know the church]; and because the church is a supernatural and mystical body, supernatural faith and the grace of God are required for knowing it.

X. One must distinguish between [1] absolute necessity and [2] relative necessity. The Word of God is absolutely and positively necessary to the church and inseparable from it. But the Sacraments are relatively and definitively necessary to the church; that is, insofar as the church is visible and able to be seen, the Word of God is chiefly and primarily a mark of the church, but the Sacraments, as appendices to the Word, δευτέρως [secondarily] and secondarily. And hence when the use of the Sacraments, e.g., of the Eucharist, lapses, namely in time of persecution, the church nevertheless remains.

XI. One must distinguish between [1] what ὄντως [really] belongs to something and [2] what belongs to it φαινομένως [apparently]; likewise, truth of a matter is one thing and the vain persuasion of people is another; likewise, it is one thing to boast of purity and truth of doctrine and it is another truly to have it. Heretics and sectarians boast of purity and truth of doctrine but do not have it. The question is not what this one or that one thinks is his, but what really belongs to him. [This] with regard to that [statement] of Bellarmine: "Pure preaching of the Word is a mark very common to all sects, at least in their own opinion."

XII. Bellarmine argues thus: "Marks ought to be better known than the thing [that is] marked. Now, the pure preaching of the Word is not better known than the church, because (1) no one can know where the Word is truly believed; (2) we learn from the church what true preaching is, just as also (3) we recognize what the true interpretation of the Scriptures is from the testimony of the church." We reply: (1) by distinguishing between what is better known by nature and what is better known to us. Thus inner and essential causes and qualities are better known by nature, but to us nonessential qualities[16] and effects are better known. We here seek such marks as provide sure and unquestioned knowledge. Such [marks] are therefore to be sought from those that are better known by nature, namely from inner causes and qualities. For, from the things by which something is constituted and preserved, from them it is also recognized beyond doubt. Now, the church is constituted and preserved by the pure preaching of the Word and the proper administration of the Sacraments. Ergo. In brief: One thing is better known ἡμῖν [to us], and another is better known τῇ φύσει [by nature]; some is confused knowledge, and some [is] distinct; γνωριμώτερα τῇ φύσει [things (that are) better known by nature] provide true and distinct knowledge, but γνωριμώτερα ἡμῖν [things (that are) better known to us] [provide] only confused [knowledge]. The Word of God is φύσει γνωριμώτερον [by nature known better] than the church, because it is the cause that constitutes and gathers the church; and because the principle and cause that constitutes and gathers the church is the Word of God, therefore the Word of God is a proper, infallible, and sure mark of the church. (2) Though we cannot point out in particular those who receive the proclaimed Word by faith, yet we certainly can say that wherever the Word of God is proclaimed there always are some who embrace it from the heart. (3) What the true preaching and explanation of Scripture is we know from the church ministerially and δευτέρως [secondarily]. (4) Unless, then, it is previously altogether clear from Scripture that this one or that one is the true church, its testimony does not generate sure persuasion or knowledge but only opinion and conjecture. Therefore it is necessary that you first be sure that a church holds the pure and true Word of God before you firmly believe its testimony.

XIII. Bellarmine objects further: "True marks are inseparable from the church. Now, in the church of the Corinthians and of the Galatians there was at times not the pure preaching of the Word, because among the Corinthians it was taught that there is no future resurrection; and among the Galatians the law of Moses was observed." We reply: (1) Not all Corinthians, but only some, held that view, 1 Cor. 15:12. the same is to be said of the Galatians, Gal. 1:7: "There are some who trouble you." (2) There are degrees of purity; sometimes the Word is preached more purely, sometimes less [purely].

XIV. Observe: We do not deny that some marks assigned by the papists apply in some times of the church, but that they apply at all times to the true church, and in particular [to it] alone and are therefore genuine, sure, and infallible marks, this we deny.

XV. Tirinus and other papists cry out and strongly protest that we reject the marks of the church of Christ that the Apostles', Nicene, and Athanasian creeds assign to it, which say that the church is one, holy, catholic, and apostolic. We reply: (1) We also ascribe these characterizations to the true church; but not everything that is attributed to the church is a mark of it. (2) Unity is not a mark that serves to distinguish one thing from another. For man is not distinguished from a monkey by unity but by reason and the ability to laugh. (3) Those assemblies that dispute the signs of the church among themselves have each its unity, which therefore is the more unfit to mark the church. (4) Unity without truth is mere vanity. When the world was of one tongue, Gen. 11:1, all combined to build the tower of Babel. And [Gregory of] Nazianzus says: "Disagreement that has arisen by reason of piety is better than sinful harmony." (5) We acknowledge that the church should be holy; but the norm and rule of establishing and recognizing true holiness is Holy Scripture alone. (6) Catholicism or universality is not a perceptible mark of the church, since universals do not strike the senses. (7) For the one Roman church to claim catholicism for itself [is] not only absurd—since it is itself particular, not universal—but also disparaging of all other churches that are older than the Roman [church] and more celebrated than the saints and holy teachers, though they [these churches] do not observe fellowship with it [the Roman church]. For the church to be apostolic requires only consanguinity of doctrine, as Tertullian says. Now, the Roman curia does not have apostolic but apostatic doctrine, 1 Tim. 4:1-2; 2 The. 2:3 f.

Notes:

1. *legitimus.*
2. *Codice Biblico.*
3. *adequatas.*
4. *Jerichunte.*
5. *Ecclesia ipsa notius.*
6. *Ecclesia.*
7. *dignitas.*
8. *regula.*
9. *evidentior.*
10. *praelucet* with the dative.
11. *synagogae.*
12. *haud paulo sanctiores.*
13. An antipope.
14. *a priori.*
15. *a posteriori.*
16. *accidentia.*

Question V

Is the Roman pontiff the absolute ruler and head of the catholic church?

The Point at Issue

I. The question is not whether Christ is the King and Head of His church, for the papists do not deny this. (II) The question is not whether the Roman pontiff is head of the whole church in the sense in which Christ is, namely life-giving and saving. (III) The question is not whether the Roman pope has primacy of order and therefore outranks the other bishops, for this was pointed out at length from antiquity by Claudius Smalcius, and those on our side have never denied this. But this is the question: (I) Whether besides Christ or under Christ there ought to be some visible absolute ruler who alone rules the universal church on earth and is the head of the whole church. And (II) whether the Roman pope is ordained by Christ [to be] the visible head and absolute ecumenical ruler of the catholic church.

Thesis

Christ alone is the King, absolute Ruler, and Head of the universal church, and we do not recognize another ecumenical and visible head of the church besides Him. For nowhere in the New Testament is it established either by Christ or by the apostles that monarchic government and the highest rule of the whole church should be in the hands of one person on this earth who would be its visible head and absolute ruler. Neither was

Peter nor is the Roman pope the ecumenical head of the catholic church or the vicar of Christ on earth.

Exposition

I. Observe: This does not come into controversy, whether there is any way of governing the church. For since the church is the household of God, 1 Tim. 3:15, in which the pastors are made the stewards of the divine mysteries, 1 Cor. 4:1, surely that house will have its own economy.

II. It is necessary that the true and genuine head of the church not only be united with the church, rise up over [it], and rule [it], but also sufficiently provide for it, recognize the needs of all the members, know [their] apprehensions, hear [their] prayers, be able to resolve [their] difficulties, [and] finally be able to bestow the Holy Spirit, grace, life, [and] affection and be able to grant spiritual understanding to all members; but this belongs to no one but Christ. Now, the pope is not always united with the church, but, according to Gerson, can be removed by it; nor is there actually always such a head, since the Roman see is often vacant, much less can it give the church the other things.

III. The papists distinguish between [1] a primary and [2] a secondary or vicarious head of the church, between an invisible and a visible head; between a head with Christ and a head under Christ. For they do not outright deny that Christ is the Head of the church, but because He removed His visible presence from us by His ascension, they require also a visible head subordinate to Him. But the apostle, 1 Cor. 3:11, makes Christ not the primary but the sole foundation of the church. These are the words of Bellarmine: "No injury derives to Christ from this, that the pope is the head of the church; in fact, His glory rather grows. For," he adds, "we do not say that the pope is the head of the church with Christ, but under Christ, as His servant and vicar." But (1) a vicar is given only to him who because of either absence or debility and inability cannot be in charge of his own matters. Neither of this fits Christ, as is clear from Mat.

28:18 [and] 20. (2) A vicar is one who, in the place of another, does not perform his own function. Now, the pope does not play into the work of Christ, except insofar as he is ἀντίχριστος [the Antichrist]. (3) If there is any vicariate of Christ in the church, it should be associated not with some particular person but by all means with all bishops and pastors.

IV. Observe: The distinction between lord and subject, between master and servant, [and] between the bridegroom of the church and his friend is in harmony with Scripture, Mat. 23:10; John 3:29; 1 Cor. 3:5. But the papists prescribe for us such a vicar and servant as is the bridegroom of the church to the exclusion of Christ, and the rock of the foundation, who, notwithstanding the instruction of Christ, may decree something else [and] from whose mouth the faithful demand more instruction than from the sacred pages of the Christian religion. "Surely," says Bellarmine, "if the church that is on earth is well compared to a spouse, with Christ hidden, also with Christ hidden it should have one head." However, a friend of the bridegroom and paranymph can be acquired,[1] but not in the same way a vicarious bridegroom or joint rival.

V. One must distinguish between [1] the position that the pontiff creates and [2] the pretext under which he imposes upon and makes sport of the church. He calls himself a servant of servants, but in fact he wants to be lord of lords, top of the bishops, [and] foundation of faith.

VI. We do not deny that there are distinct orders of servants in the church, nor do we raise questions regarding the primacy of order with regard to outward economy, but we deny that the monarchic rule belongs to one pontiff and that he is properly called the head of the church, to whom belongs, by divine right, the highest and absolute canonical, decisive, legislative, and jurisdictional power.

VII. One must distinguish between a successor of Peter (1) in the pontificate, (2) his successor in the apostolate, and (3) his successor in the office of preaching the Gospel. Peter had no successor, properly speaking, either in the pontificate, which he never had, or in the apostolate, in which succession is not given, but in the office of preaching the Gospel. And in this all true pastors are successors of the apostles.

VIII. One must distinguish between succession by right and succession in fact. The succession of Peter that the pope claims for himself is not by right but in fact.

IX. Observe: προεδρία [precedence] or primacy of order among bishops belongs to the Roman bishop mostly out of respect for the city of Rome, which, just as foremost and chief in the world, so it also had a bishop superior to the others in rank.

X. Observe: There is no passage of Holy Scripture from which it is clear that Peter was ever in Rome. And though we admit that Peter was in Rome, yet we steadfastly deny that the same exercised monarchic rule for 25 years there in the papal see, as the papists say, especially Bellarmine and others. For as the papists could never show that Peter sat at Antioch seven years, before the second [year] of Claudius, in which, [as] they would have it, Peter came to Rome, so now they could never prove that his Roman episcopate lasted 25 years. Petavius assigns that departure of Peter to Rome to the third [year] of Claudius, in fact Baronius himself begins the first year of Peter with the third [year] of Claudius, not with the second, as [do] Tirinus and others. But now, the third [year] of Claudius to the fourteenth of Nero, in which they would have Peter suffering martyrdom, are not 25 years—to say nothing of the fact that to turn the apostles into bishops of particular churches would be to deprive them of their high position of the apostolate.

Antithesis

Of the papists, who subordinate to Christ the Roman pope as supreme ruler and universal head of the church and make him the vicar of Christ on earth beyond and contrary to Scripture. For they teach (I) that he is a sort of visible head of the church militant on earth [and] (II) that the Roman pope himself is established by divine right and by Christ Himself as head, chief, and supreme ruler of the church, with authority infallibly to determine and define matters of faith. For so [says] Bellarmine: "Even though Christ is the sole and proper King and Supreme Ruler of the Catholic Church and rules and governs it spiritually and invisibly, yet the church, which is physical and visible, needs some one visible highest judge by whom disputes that have arisen about religion might be settled and who might contain all lower prefects in office and unity." Franciscus Turrianus says: "The kingdom of Christ on this earth is the supreme rule of the Roman Catholic Church, etc. And if the Catholic Church is the monarchy of Christ, which is visible, then Christ chose in it the supreme ruler, who also would be visible." Salmerõn [says]: "Just as God over creatures, Adam in mankind, the head in an animal body, [and] a commander over troops, so God wanted one to be the highest shepherd and supreme ruler in the church, whom all others would obey." Coster [says]: "We hold that one shepherd was the head of the church, who in his turn ruled the church." The Jesuit Tirinus writes: "Christ substituted a particular person as vicar for Himself on earth, who would be the supreme head and spiritual monarch of the whole church (though all heretics loudly protest); we surely gather from this that he established His church in the best way like troops in array, SSo. 6:4[2]." And Bellarmine tried at great length to prove that the Roman pope himself is the universal head and monarch of the church. Abraham Bzovius exalts the Roman pope that way in all 50 chapters [of his book on the Roman papacy] and calls him the monarch of Christians, chosen[3] by God, the highest of mortals, the head of the Catholic Church. Barthold Nihus says: "For us Catholics (papists) nothing else is certain but that the Roman popes were of old made heads of the whole militant church in St. Peter by Christ Himself, and such they also always were until now and will be to the end of the world. And this our simple faith suffices us, and it does not rest on or need proofs." The primacy and rule of the pope [is] therefore to be believed, not to be proved, according to what Nihus thinks.[4] Augustinus Triumphus and Alvar Pelayo hold: "The chief pontiff has absolutely complete power by divine right in the whole world, both in ecclesiastical and in political matters."

In fact, in the Lateran Council, Sess. 4, the pope lent favorable ear to Christopher Marcellus, who said: "You are another God on earth."

Confirmation of the Thesis

We prove that Christ is the true and μοναδικὸν [sole] or only head of the catholic church

I. From the Holy Scriptures, from which it is clear that Christ was made King, Shepherd, Ruler, and Head of the church by God. For thus says the apostle, Eph. 1:22-23: "He has put all things under His feet and gave Him as Head over all things to the church itself, which is His body, the fullness of Him who fills all in all." And Col. 1:18: "He is the Head of the body, the church, who is the beginning, the firstborn from the dead, that in all things He might have the primacy." Cf. Eph. 4:15; 5:23. And certainly, as there is one body and one Spirit, so also [is there] one Head, especially since Christ is the Head of the church in the same way as a husband [is the head of his] wife, who [the husband] does not let a vicar into the marital role. "One king, one monarch, one sole head," says Gregory I, "ἡ μία καὶ μόνα ἀληθῶς κεφαλὴ [the one and sole truly head]," says Basil, or whoever is their author, in *Asceticis*. Only Christ is the leader of the army of God, Jos. 5:14. The sole οἰκοδεσπότης [master of a house] and head of a household, Mat. 10:25; 21:33; Heb. 3:6. The sole head of the mystic body, Col. 1:18; 2:19. The king and monarch of this kingdom, Rev. 19:12, 16; ἀρχιποιμὴν [chief shepherd] and Good Shepherd of this sheepfold, John 10:11, 14; Heb. 13:20; 1 Ptr. 5:4. The same is described [in terms] of wisdom, righteousness, and good government, Jer. 23:5: "A king will reign and do wisely and well and execute judgment and justice on earth." Cf. Psa. 2:6. Whomever therefore God in [His] most wise counsel made Head, King, Shepherd, and all-sufficient Ruler of the church and whom He set before it to be solely embraced, with an added caution about the need to flee the enemy, who assumes the principle of head in the church, He alone is the true Head of the church and

113

is alone to be acknowledged as the Head. Now, Jesus Christ is He whom God made the Head of the church in that way. Ergo.

II. From the requisites of the true Head, which so attach to Christ as to no one else, (1) for Christ is most closely joined to the church, not only as God but also as man, by [His] substantial, singular, [and] gracious presence, to this extent, that the church is called "σῶμα καὶ πλήρομα, the body and fullness of Him who fills all in all," Eph. 1:23, and we individually are called "members of His body, of His flesh, and of His bones," Eph. 5:30. (2) He Himself, in the same way as a head is in charge of the whole body, rules and provides, knows, attends, and provides for all the needs of those who are His own, perceives sighings, hears prayers, [and] tempers the affairs of the pious according to His good pleasure, so that all things work together for good for those who love God. (3) In the manner of a head He imparts to His body the Holy Spirit and vital powers, life, spiritual disposition and understanding, and all things necessary for spiritual life; regarding this matter the words of the apostle, Eph. 4:15–16, are highly significant: "Let us in all things grow up in Him, Christ, who is the Head, from whom the whole body, compacted and knit together διὰ πάσης ἁφῆς τῆς ἐπιχορηγίας, by the connection supplied by all [ligaments], κατ᾽ ἐνέργειαν, according to the operation in the measure of every part, makes increase of the body for its upbuilding in love." Observe: If the monarchic rule of Christ in the kingdom of the saints is established in such a way that He is the Head of the whole mystical body at all times [and under all] states and local conditions, He is the sole Ruler and Head, incompossible and incompatible with another, visible monarch and head in that worldwide kingdom. Otherwise the church would not be a well-ordered body but a monster and two-headed, in fact multiheaded. You say: "The mystic body of Christ would be monstrous if it would have two equal heads, but the papists do not say that; they specify one head primary, the other secondary." We reply: The monstrous form is not avoided in that way, for a primary and a secondary head nevertheless makes two heads and form a monster. You insist: "It is not ours to speak of the monstrous form of the church on the analogy of natural bodies, since necessity and the nature of the church require this, that besides a primary head it have also a secondary head. Necessity demands this because of the lack of the visible presence of Christ; hence the church must be kept in unity by a visible head." We reply: (1) We rightly advance the analogy of natural bodies here; it is twofold here: For Christ alone is the Head of the church (a) by reason of quickening, for it is quickened and made alive by Him and receives spiritual understanding and disposition [from Him]; (b) by reason of government, for it is ruled and governed by Him as a body [is ruled] by [its] head. (2) There is no need of a visible ecumenical head to keep unity, both [1] because unity consists fundamentally and basically in invisible and divine union, for which a visible presence does not suffice, and [2] because invisible presence is infinitely sufficient and effective for that invisible συναγμολογίαν [unity]. (3) For the king to have a vicegerent is of imperfection, because he can be with all inhabitants of his realm neither invisibly nor visibly. (4) Whoever therefore gives the church all things that are of the Head, with regard to both means and end, and is always and everywhere present with it, He is the Head of the church in such a way that it needs no other. Now, Christ etc. Ergo.

III. From reasons, of which (1) is drawn from the silence of Scripture. We do not read that Christ was made an ecclesiastical monarch who would maintain His substitute parts on earth, but He committed and entrusted the care of the church equally to the apostles, Mat. 28:19-20; John 20:21, 23. In fact, He rather rejected clearly monarchical rule of any person in the church, Luke 22:24-26. (2) From the unity of the church, which Scripture always derives from the unity of Christ the Head and of the Holy Spirit, Rom. 1:5; Gal. 3:28. (3) From the presence of Christ. For Christ is always very present with His church, Mat. 28:19, and therefore does not need a vicar on earth. (4) From the betrothal of the church. He that is the Head of the church, the same is also its Bridegroom. Now, the church does not recognize two bridegrooms, lest it commit adultery, nor two heads, lest it become a two-headed monster.

One must observe here that Christ did not make the apostles vicars and locum tenentes of His royal majesty, but διακονίας [of service], which He Himself performed among the Jewish people in the days of [His] flesh, with πάσῃ ἐξοθσίᾳ [all power] in heaven and on earth reserved to Himself, Mat. 28:18. Thus the whole authority[5] of the apostles will have been ministerial. "As My Father has sent Me, so I send you," John 20:21. Now, He was sent as a servant or minister of [the] circumcision or to perform personal service among the Jewish people, Rom. 15:8. Hence also the apostles claimed no other title for themselves than that of ministry.

And that the Roman pope is not the true head of the church we prove from the lack of a call and of institution. For the Jesuits can bring nothing from Holy Scripture regarding the institution of a vicarious head, much less can they prove from Scripture that the Roman pope is such a vicarious and secondary head. We argue thus: (1) "Every true head of the church is instituted by God or [by] Christ θεανθρώπῳ [the God-man], received by the early church, and appointed in the description of the ecclesiastical hierarchy. Now then, the Roman pontiff is not instituted by God or [by] Christ θεανθρώπῳ [the God-man], nor received by the early church, nor appointed in the description of the ecclesiastical hierarchy. Therefore the Roman pontiff is not the true head of Christ's church." Certainly Bellarmine tries to prove that both by divine right and by reason of succession the Roman pontiff is Peter's successor in the ecclesiastical monarchy, but even so he does not want to prove that Christ Himself directly connected the primacy of Peter with the city and episcopate of Rome; in fact, he acknowledges that it is not [required to be held as an article] of faith, as some say, that Peter moved his see to Rome by divine command after leaving Antioch, and he clearly says that we do not know how Christ commanded Peter to establish [his] see at Rome. (2) "What none of the apostles had or exercised, the Roman pope should not arrogate to himself. Now, none of the apostles had or exercised rule over the church. Ergo." The minor [premise] is proved: Peter and the rest of the apostles never, not even as far as title, arrogated to themselves the rule over the whole church, much less actually exercised [it]. Ergo. (3) "What conflicts with the nature of the ecclesiastical ministry, this the Roman pontiff ought to regard as foreign to himself. Now, primacy conflicts with the nature of the ecclesiastical ministry. Ergo." The minor [premise] is proved, because (a) Luke 22:25[–26] and 1 Ptr. 5:3: τὸ κυριεύειν [to rule] is forbidden to the ministers of the church, and Christ Himself committed not ἀρχὴν [sovereignty] or magistracy properly so called, but οἰκονομίαν [stewardship], διακονίαν [service], and ministry. (b) Ministry and mastery conflict; and according to Origen, on Isa. 6: "A bishop is called not to the primacy but to the service of the church." Observe: From Mat. 18:1 and Luke 22:24 it is clear that the disciples argued among themselves τίς ἄρα μείζων ἐν βασιλείᾳ τῶν οὐρανῶν, who is the greatest in the kingdom of heaven; or, as the Lord puts it, who is πρῶτος [Mark 9:35] or first, that is, as to ecclesiastical primacy in the kingdom of grace. Now, the Savior completely rejected this practice as foreign to the function of the apostles, saying: "The kings of the Gentiles exercise lordship—but you not so," etc. Bellarmine objects: "With those words the Lord does not flatly forbid dominion to bishops, but tyrannical dominion, since in Mat. 20:25 and 1 Ptr. 5:3 it is κατακυριεύειν [to exercise lordship], that is, to rule violently, and therefore it is forbidden to rule after the manner of kings and princes." We reply: (a) Christ deprives His disciples not only of [the act of] ruling but of dominion itself. Therefore He forbids them not only tyrannical but any kind of civil rule. (b) Christ denies His disciples the kind of rule they desired, but James and John as well as the rest of the disciples did not desire tyrannical rule but political rule [that is] right and compatible with the earthly kingdom of Christ that they envisioned. Therefore the Savior condemns in them the desire for political rule and for primacy of power and commends the ministry to them by His example, in that He Himself "came διακονῆσαι, to minister," etc. (c) What Matthew and Peter call κατακυριεύειν [to exercise lordship] and κατεξοθσιάζειν [to exercise authority over], Luke simply calls κυριεύειν [to be lord of] and ἐξουσιάζειν [to exercise authority over]. Therefore one looks in vain for emphasis in composite verbs, as though they mean violent and tyrannical overlordship, since also in Acts 19:16 κατακυριεύειν is used simply for having the upper hand or prevailing. (d) St. Paul excludes not only κατακυριεύειν but also κυριεύειν from himself and the rest of the apostles, 2 Cor. 1:24. (e) Therefore, whatever is said of the kings of the Gentiles by the restriction, "but you not so," that is forbidden for disciples and ministers. Now then, overlordship or primacy of power is said of the kings of the Gentiles. Therefore primacy of power and overlordship is forbidden for ministers of the church by the restriction that is added. (4) We argue: "Whoever does not attend to relieving the needs of the church and cannot meet them, he is not the head of the church. The Roman pope does not attend to relieving the needs of the church. Ergo. (5) He whose supervision and jurisdiction from of old and by right is particular and restricted by certain limits, he is not an ecumenical or universal head. The supervision and jurisdiction of the Roman bishop, from of old and by right, is particular and restricted by certain limits. Ergo."

Refutation of Objections

I. Observe: We read that one high priest was given to the Jews in the Old Testament, but it is not true that they were restricted to one priest (as we read regarding rendering obedience in Deu. 19), because the people were commanded (1) to go to the Levitical priests, not commanded to go to one high [priest], v. 9; (2) to do according to the direction of the judgment that they render and to observe to do as they teach, vv. 10–11; (3) not to depart from the judgment that they render, v. 11. We also read of many things instituted in the Old Testament that did not need to be in the New. It is therefore not valid to argue from the Old to the New. Moreover, besides the Priest in heaven the church of the Old Testament had a high priest on earth, but not the church of the New Testament. For [the church of] the Old Testament had a visible high priest, because the Old Testament or Jewish high priest was a figure and type of Christ, the true ἀρχιερέως [high priest] as well as [the true] ἱερείου [sacrifice] and that salutary sacrifice whose shadow the Jews once had, [but] we today have the body [lit. the truth; cf. Col. 2:17]. Now, when the fulfillment comes, the types cease.

II. Observe: If Christ put one ecumenical high priest and head in charge of the church, he would have to be in the apostolical hierarchy. For the apostles no doubt had such as Christ established, unless you would say that they either did not know the ordinance of Christ or did not want to observe [it], of which the former is absurd, the latter even blasphemous. Now, in the apostolical hierarchy there was not an ecumenical high priest and head of the whole church. For in Eph. 4:11–12 Paul mentions with highest trustworthiness the levels of hierarchical order appointed and equipped with gifts for the work of the ministry. And not one among them is that ecumenical one.

III. They object: "The primacy was promised to Peter, Mat. 16:18 ('You are Peter,' etc.) and therefore to the Roman pope, and it was conferred [on him] in John 21 ('Feed My sheep')." We reply: (1) The statement in Mat. 16:18, "You are Peter" etc. does not apply here. For *Petrus* [Peter] and *Petra* [Rock] are different. By *Petram* [Rock] is meant not Peter but either Peter's confession or Christ, who alone is the rock on which the church should be built [and] who was confessed by Peter. But if some fathers also give Peter the name "Rock," they do this in a metonymic sense common also to the other disciples; hence Jerome [says]: "The rock is Christ, who gave to all the apostles that they also be called rocks." None of the fathers imagines anything about a monarchy of Peter, promised him by this metaphor; Casaubon convincingly points this out over against Baronius. (2) This metaphor is drawn from the solidity and firmness of the Rock, not from overlordship, which is not in Peter. The Rock is therefore not a symbol of overlordship, not even in Christ. Therefore Baronius, Bellarmine, Maldonatus, and other champions of papal omnipotence are deceived, who try to prove from this passage that Christ made Peter the rock, keystone, foundation, ruler, and monarch of His church. Maldonatus objects: "The demonstrative *this* ('on this Rock') is put in the place of a relative, and it is the same as if He had said: 'You are the Rock on which I will build My church.'" We reply: (1) How is a relative of the feminine gender referred to an antecedent of a different gender? Certainly *hanc* [a feminine relative] and *Petrus* [a masculine name] are not of one and the same gender. (2) The fathers refer the pronoun *this* not to Peter but to the faith or confession of Peter [that is] contained in a preceding verse. (3) The pronoun ταύτῃ [this] either has the force of a relative or it is taken δεικτικῶς, that is, demonstratively. If you take it for a relative, it is referred either to the confession of faith made by Peter or to Christ Himself, the Rock of Salvation. If you take [it] demonstratively, it is taken of the very person who is speaking. After Christ had said, "You are Peter," He does not continue with these words, "and on you, Peter, I will build My church," but, with the noun and the pronoun changed, He says, "ἐπί ταύτῃ τῇ πέτρᾳ, on this rock I will build" etc., indicating very clearly that He speaks of a different rock than Peter, whom He soon in the chapter, verse 23, calls Satan.

IV. The papists also try to prove that Christ made Peter the one ecumenical sole high priest and visible head of the whole church from this, that He promised Peter the keys of the kingdom of heaven. We reply: (1) by distinguishing between the way in which Peter has the keys of the kingdom of heaven and the way in which Christ has the keys of David. Christ shuts in such a way that no one can open, and He opens in such a way that no one can close, Rev. 3:7. Now, Christ gave Peter the keys as to a subordinate servant and steward in the house of God. And a ruler who appoints a steward in [his] house does not give him a free hand in all things but only power to administer household matters, and that [power] not absolute but limited by certain rules. (2) The papists are inept when they try to prove from those words in Mat. 16:19, "I will give you the keys of the kingdom of heaven" etc. that the highest ecclesiastical power or supreme judgment regarding matters of faith was given only to Peter and his successors. For by keys is designated the ordinary power of the ministry to loose and to bind that was both promised and conferred equally to all the apostles, but not the highest ecclesiastical power, Mat. 18:18. The same keys were given with the same broad terminology equally to all the apostles: "Whatsoever you will bind on earth" etc. Here, with the definition of a key given, that which is defined is also put. (3) The keys are not given to Peter and his successors as to a lord, so that he might use them αὐτοκρατικῶς [autocratically] and freely, but as to a steward and minister, as stated in 1 Cor. 4:1; 1 Tim. 3:15; Mat. 13:52[6], who is held to adapt their use to the command and will of the Lord. Ecclesiastical power is not αὐτοκρατορικὴ [autocratic], inasmuch as that belongs only to Christ, but ministerial and limited. (4) The keys were not only given to Peter but also to the rest of the apostles; for just as, when all are asked, one replies in the name of all, Mat. 16:15–16; John 6:67–69, so are the keys committed to all in the one. For, given to all, they are used equally by all, as Scripture says, Mat. 18:18; John 20:23. The keys were not given to one [*uni*] but to the unity [*unitati*], as the fathers put it.

V. They object that Christ entrusted to Peter alone, as to the ecumenical shepherd and administrative head after the resurrection not some but all lambs and sheep to feed, and that for the third time, John 21:15–17, and thus entrusted to him and his successors the care and government of the whole church. And the papists emphasize these three things most of all: (1) "Feed My sheep" is said only to Peter. (2) By the word "feed" is meant the highest power and absolute rule. And (3) the sheep of Christ here are the whole church, also the apostles themselves. We reply: (1) Peter is called three times to feed the sheep, so that by a triple confession he might as it were wash out the blot of [his] triple denial. (2) What was once said only to Peter does not apply only to Peter. One must prove that something special given to Peter [was] not [given] to the rest in common with him. (3) What Christ here said to Peter in figurative and metaphorical words ("Feed My sheep") this He elsewhere commanded all the apostles in proper words ("Teach all nations"), Mat. 28:19; Mark 16:15. Something special is therefore not bestowed on Peter here. Hence Augustine says: "Inasmuch as it is said to

Peter, it is said to all, 'Do you love Me? Feed My sheep.'" In fact all the apostles are called shepherds, Jer. 3:15. And the rest of the teachers of the church are also commanded to feed the flock of Christ, 1 Ptr. 5:2; Acts 20:28. (4) The function of feeding is here given to Peter, not ruling power. For, you see, "Feed the sheep of Christ" is not the same as to rule the sheep of Christ, much less to lord it over shepherds as well as sheep, and that with highest power. In the proper sense indeed τὸ [the word] "feed" designates every pastoral act. But taken metaphorically, the meaning must be determined ἀναλόγως [fittingly] to the subject that is spoken of, for a bishop feeds the flock of Christ in one way, a king [his] subjects in another way. Therefore, just as in a king it does not mean that he should feed [his] subjects with the preaching of the Word and the administration of the Sacraments, so in a bishop it does not mean that he should rule the church. Feeding a flock is done by teaching, not ruling, decreeing, or commanding. (5) If ποιμαίνειν [feeding] is the same as overlording, it follows that all bishops and ministers of the church are monarchs, since all are commanded ποιμαίνειν [to feed] the church, Acts 20:28. (6) In the passage cited, St. John twice uses the word βόσκειν [feed], vv. 15 and 17, which does not mean rule but nutrition, [and] he uses the word ποιμαίνειν [lead to pasture] once, v. 16, so that we are to seek no absolute rule here, but we are to understand that ποιμαίνειν like βόσκειν are here to be taken in the same sense. (7) ποιμαίνειν used of a king indeed means to feed by ruling, but not the same of a minister of the church. (8) The Savior very strictly forbids the apostles to rule, Mat. 20:25–26; Mark 10:42–43; Luke 22:25–26. Cf. the Confirmation [of the thesis]. (9) And what is more inept than the argument of Bellarmine: Because the Roman pope preaches neither by writing nor speaking, therefore τὸ [the word] "feed" is the same as command and decree, which is to be believed. Much more correctly it is implied: therefore the Roman pope clearly does not feed the sheep of Christ, as Bernhard writes to Eugene IV: To evangelize is to feed. Either deny yourself [to be] a shepherd to the people or show [yourself to be one]. (10) How do the papists prove that by "sheep" in the passage cited are meant the whole church, or simply all Christians, including also the apostles themselves? Surely if the care of absolutely all the sheep of Christ had been thus committed to Peter, so that he alone with his successors was to feed the flock of the Lord, the rest of the apostles would have been idle. It was said equally to all, Mat. 28:19, "Having gone out, teach all nations," and the very truth wrings this statement out of Bellarmine. All the apostles were heads, leaders, and shepherds of the whole church. It was said in a general way to Peter, "Feed My sheep"; all sheep were not entrusted to him universally. And Peter did not feed all the sheep of Christ. He did not feed the apostles by teaching (for they were all equally taught by the Holy Spirit), not by correction (for one reads this nowhere; in fact, Paul corrected him, Gal. 2:11), [and] not by ruling over them (for they were equals in the apostolate). Nor did he feed all the rest of the sheep of Christ, for he did not get to all. Bellarmine also looks for a hidden meaning in the words ἀρνίων [lambs] and προβάτων [sheep], but lambs and sheep are often taken for the same in Scripture, as is clear from a comparison of the passages in Mat. 10:16 [and] Luke 10:3; cf. Zec. 11:4. And this variation involves no hidden meaning in this passage, as the more learned papists themselves admit. Christ entrusts lambs and sheep equally to Peter to feed, not that He makes him a shepherd of shepherds, who is to feed children and women [and] rule both subjects and prelates, but that in the person of Peter He exhorts all shepherds and that the tender and weak should be nourished with milk like lambs and sheep, as the more perfect, are to be well taken care of, as Ambrose says: "With these words, 'Feed My sheep,' the Savior committed nothing more to Peter than the ecclesiastical office that He committed equally also to the other apostles."

VI. Observe: From 1 Cor. 12:21, where Paul says that such a head is given to the church as cannot say to the feet, "I do not need you," Tirinus tries to prove that an invisible head is not enough for the visible church. We reply: From this passage one cannot gather the need of a visible head in the universal church. For (1) Paul does not take the head that cannot say to the feet, "I do not need you," formally, but only materially, for a member more noble than another, so that he might rather point out the connection and mutual need of all members; and that is clear from this, that in the same place he distinguishes the ears and eyes from the head, even though they belong to the head formally considered. (2) The whole church is there described by Paul as the body of Christ (not of the pope), who is its Head, as Cornelius a Lapide says on 1 Cor. 12:12.

VII. Observe: When Paul draws a comparison with a body and posits Christ as its sole Head, he does not draw a comparison with some body [that is] also political, such as is a kingdom, which can allow for a king and a vicegerent, but with a natural and human body, which, if it have another head besides the human [head], is a two-headed body and a monster.

VIII. They object: "Monarchic rule is excellent and the best and noblest form of governing, by which one is over all. Therefore this befits the church as altogether perfect and best constituted." We reply: One must distinguish between government regarded [1] absolutely and as such, and in that way no government and no monarchy can be called excellent; and [2] regarded in respect to the subject to be ruled and the circumstances, and in that way that government is best which is best suited to the subjects to be ruled and in respect to the circumstances. A government that in itself is outstanding is not always better or more beneficial for this or that subject. There are people who cannot be ruled in any other way than μοναρχικῶς [monarchically], [and] there are others who cannot bear the rule of one. Therefore monarchical rule is not suitable for ruling just any multitude. For some are ruled more easily and more successfully aristocratically than monarchically, and others better democratically than monarchically. The universal church is not a society visibly one; therefore one singular role of one monarch cannot be the best for the whole church.

IX. Bellarmine advances some canons of councils, but one must distinguish between universal rule and προεδρίαν or primacy of order. The canons of councils and some fathers ascribe the latter, not the former, to the bishops of the city of Rome. In the council of Carthage and Hippo it was decreed that the bishop of a primary see not be called head of the priests. In [the council] of Mileve: "Let no appeal be made out of Africa across the sea to Rome." In [the council] of Chalcedon and the second [council] of Constantinople: "Let the bishop of Constantinople be extolled with the one of Rome." They insist: "The council of Nicaea decreed that, if the ordinary judges were suspect, all bishops should freely appeal to the apostolic see; the letter of Athanasius to Pope Felix cites this canon." We reply: That canon is spurious, as [is] that letter of Athanasius, which contains many false and worthless things. There are only 20 canons of Nicaea, [and] in them [there is] nothing about appeals to Rome. In fact, in canons 5 and 6 all appeal to the Roman pope is clearly excluded. They insist: "There are various examples of appeals to the pope." We reply: Some of those who appealed were heretics, others took recourse to Rome only to get help, because the Roman church was still orthodox. The papists insist: A few years after the Council of Nicaea, in the Council of Sardica, it was decreed, as Hosius writes, that one could lay a matter regarding controversies before the Roman pope. We reply: (1) This council was not ecumenical. (2) Canons 4 and 7 of Sardica conflict with [canons] 5 and 6 of the Council of Nicaea. (3) These canons were not accepted by the whole Western Church. (4) And the canons of Sardica do not ascribe the right of appeal or of highest power to the Roman pope.

X. Bellarmine also advances testimonies of Roman popes, but (1) as witnesses in their own interest they are not justified. (2) From those testimonies it appears not so much that they had, as that they claimed and assumed ruling power. The pope does not have the power of right, which he sought by action or tyranny. (3) Those who embraced the title of universal bishop, Pope Gregory accuses of anti-Christianity. And Origen says: "A bishop is not called to rule but to serve the church."

XI. Bellarmine also argues on the basis of the names of the Roman popes, which are pope, father of fathers, high priest, high priest of Christians, prince of priests, vicar of Christ, teacher of all the faithful, foundation of the building of the church, bridegroom of the church, [and] universal bishop. We reply: (1) Those names originate partly with the superstitious supporters of the Roman see, [and] partly they have also been ascribed to other teachers of the churches. For Athanasius is called prefect of the catholic church; Chrysostom, teacher of the world; Cyprian, Augustine, Alypius, [and] Euphronius (bishop of Tours), popes and pontiffs. In fact, the name "pope" was of old common to all bishops, as is certainly clear from Athanasius, Epiphanius, Eusebius, Sidonius, Apollinaris, and other writers. Epiphanius is called ecumenical patriarch, Athanasius[7] [is called] general patriarch, etc. (2) At the time of the apostles no one recognized the bishop of Rome as the foundation and head of the whole church, [and] after the time of the apostles, though the Roman bishop was [held] in honor, yet for the first five centuries and somewhat longer he was not recognized as sole ecumenical pontiff by the holy fathers. A letter of a council to Leo calls him pope, but that letter is scarcely genuine, so far as one gathers from [the letter] itself and the action of the council. And the title of head is not a mark of highest jurisdiction, but of order, of which mention is clearly made in the letter.

XII. The papists object: "Because the head of the church always sat and still sits in Rome, the Roman church is called the mother and head of all churches by Anacletus, Felix, Cyprian, Ambrose, [and] Augustine." We reply: (1) It is false, that the Roman church is the mother of all the rest. Just as the Greek church received the faith from [the church] of Jerusalem, so did the Roman [church] from the Greek [church], rather than the latter from the former. Therefore [the church of] Jerusalem is the mother of all churches. See Isa. 2:3; Mic. 4:2; Luke 24:47. (2) The witnesses do not agree. Anacletus both is spurious and does not say what is said here. Felix martyr is also a spurious or false witness. Cyprian calls the root and mother of the catholic church not the catholic church as opposed to the rest of the churches outside of Rome, but as opposed to the Novatian faction and joined to Cornelius. One reads such things neither in Basil nor in Ambrose, nor are passages cited by the papists. Augustine writes: "In the Roman church the primacy," that is, the episcopate, "of the apostolic see always flourished"; so also

Leo calls the Roman church mother, but does not call [it] the mother of all churches. Augustine in many ways says that he does not recognize the Roman bishop as the one ecumenical bishop.

XIII. Observe: Though one human being can have many heads, e.g., a mystic [head] is Christ, a political [head] who is king, prince, or magistrate, [and] a marital [head] if she is a woman, and yet some monstrosity does not result from it, nevertheless one body or one human being cannot have many heads in the same order and respect without monstrosity. Thus, e.g., a woman might have three heads that are of diverse order and respect, yet cannot have two in one and the same order and respect, e.g., two marital [heads] without ceasing to be a lawful wife and degenerating into a monstrous adulteress.

XIV. Observe: It does not follow [to say]: The church is a kind of a visible body called kingdom in Dan. 2^8, sheepfold in John 10, house in 1 Tim. 3; therefore a visible head, king, shepherd, and a visible head of the household is also required. For this is not essential but accidental for the nature of a head; that is clear from this, that visibility is an accidental quality [and] an essential [quality] of a head is to rule [and] govern the body, give it a vital spirit, etc. The church is the house of God the Father and of the Holy Spirit, yet God the Father and the Holy Spirit are not therefore visible.

XV. One must distinguish between a head in the church and a head of the church. There is room for a head, indeed heads, in the church. For there is room in the church for bishops, who of old were called heads, [and] there is room for more noble and more outstanding members, as Paul himself says, 1 Cor. 12^9, but there is no room for another head besides Christ, both by reason of the influx of internal [administration] and by reason [of the influx] of outward administration and rule. After that monarchical visible head of the church, or new τέρας [portent], or monstrosity, came to light, so little good came of it for the church, that, on the contrary, from that time all things turned for the worse.

Notes:

1. *ferri.*
2. Latin text: 3. For the language cf. the Vulgate.
3. *assumptum.*
4. *ex mente Nihusii.*
5. *dignitas.*
6. Latin text: 13.
7. Latin text: Thenasius.
8. Latin text: 9.
9. Latin text: 10.

128

Question VI

Is the power to convoke councils and preside over them in the hands of the emperor, or princes, or rather in the hands of the Roman pontiff?

Thesis

I. The right and authority to convoke councils, especially ecumenical or general [councils] is not in the hands of the Roman pontiff but in the hands of the emperor or the highest political magistrate.

II. The chairman of a council is not necessarily the Roman bishop or his legate but he that is elected thereto by the votes of the bishops.

Exposition, at the same time setting forth the point at issue.

I. The question is not whether it is so necessary that a synod be convoked by a political magistrate that, when the church lacks a faithful magistrate, then either the help of the political magistrate, no matter how unbelieving, is to be used or one is to abstain altogether from the concern of convoking a council; for we readily grant that a church lacking a faithful magistrate is not held to employ the services of an unbelieving magistrate in convoking a council. We stress the apostolic practice not known to fail, for the apostles gathered without consulting the civil magistrate, in fact when he was unwilling, to choose ministers of the church, Acts 1, 6, and 13, as well as to examine the labors of ministers, Acts 11:1 ff., as to settle controversies in religion that had arisen, Acts 15:1 ff. But this comes properly into controversy: Is it the ex officio function of a political but believing magistrate to convoke councils by his edict and to do this, so that all things might be done properly in the council according to the direction of the divine Word; and this we affirm.

II. We deny the Roman pontiff not only the right and authority to convoke ecumenical councils but also that his consent is absolutely necessary for them to gather; for it is possible for the emperor to convoke a council when the pontiff is unwilling.

III. And yet the question is properly not about consent but about the power to convoke [a council]. The right and authority to convoke [a council] does not follow directly from consent, because other bishops also give consent, although because of the eminence of the city of Rome, the bishop of that place, as the foremost, would be asked regarding consent.

IV. One must distinguish between οἰκουμενικά, universal or general, and τοπικά [local], particular councils, namely national and provincial. Here the question is properly and principally not about particular but ecumenical councils.

V. The question is about the convoker, either one who definitely consents to the assembly or who later ratifies [it]. But if the emperor himself does not convoke a general council, nor [does] someone else in accordance with his order or [with his] consent, nor does he himself at least approve the call to gather, [then] that is not a lawful council but only a conciliabulum[1].

VI. Just as in all other conventions, so also in councils is there required some certain chairman and moderator, so that all things might be done "εὐσχημόνως καὶ κατὰ τάξιν [in a proper and orderly way]," 1 Cor. 14:40.

VII. One must distinguish between [1] a chairman as to τὰ ἔσω τῆς ἐκκλησίας, or the internal matters of the church, namely doctrine itself, and [2] a chairman as to τὰ ἔξω, or the outward matters and the things that make for proper order. The ordinary chairman of universal and major councils, as to outward matters, is the Christian emperor or prince or someone sent or delegated by him. But as to the internal matters of the church, or the ecclesiastical actions themselves that deal with faith and doctrine, the chairman of a council is one or more bishops [appointed] by the emperor himself or a prince or elected by the common vote of the whole council. And we have pointed out in Sect. I, Thesis XXX, cf. Thesis XXIX, that in the ecumenical and major councils several ecclesiastical chairmen were elected who guided the synodical proceedings either taking turns or together, not with compulsory but with directive authority.

VIII. Therefore there is a threefold chairman of councils: (1) God, who speaks through His Word, revealed in Holy Scripture, to those assembled in the councils in the name of Christ; (2) the emperor, or highest political magistrate, with authority and power to command, but bound to the Word of God; (3) one or more bishops surpassing others in learning, piety, the use of things, prudence, authority, and other gifts, who call for votes and state decisions.

IX. We know that in some councils the legates of the Roman bishop presided, but we deny that this is positively and absolutely necessary and that this presidency, together with papal authority and monarchical power, belongs to him.

Antithesis

Of the papists, who (I) hold that the Roman pontiff [as] putative vicar of Christ, has the power to convoke a general council. For thus [says] Julius II in the Lateran Council, Sess. 1, and in the bull of convocation: "They saw that councils are convened in this way alone by the Roman pontiffs." Salmerõn, on Acts 15: "By whose authority and command this (apostolic) council was assembled is not to be called into question, for Peter was present, the head of the apostles; by his authority alone or that of his successor can general councils be assembled." Gardillus [says]: "The power and authority to convoke, assemble, and hold an ecumenical council belongs not to the emperor but to the highest pontiff." Bellarmine [says]: "Catholics hold that the function of convoking general councils belongs to the Roman pontiff, yet in such a way that also another, with the pontiff consenting, can convoke a council, but it is also enough if he later ratifies and confirms a call that has been issued [for a council]. But if he himself does not convoke a council, nor does someone else by his command or with his consent [do so], and he himself does not at least approve the call to assemble, that will be not a council but a conciliabulum." Gregory of Valencia [says]: "A universal council that is not convoked by the universal shepherd, the Roman pontiff, is not worthy of the name 'council'." And though they finally grant a magistrate the right to convoke councils, yet that is done only by way of carrying out the will of the Roman pontiff, says Stapleton. But the Roman pontiffs claim solely to convoke councils with authority and preceptively. (II) Those who take part in presiding in general councils with plenary power to guide the council proceedings and announce decisions also defer to the Roman pontiff. Thus John of Turrecremata [says]: "According to rule, the Roman pontiff has [the prerogative] personally or [by] his legates to preside over a general council." Caspar Gardillus [says]: "In ecumenical councils only the pope[2] presides by right or those who represent him[3] in the councils." Bellarmine [says]: "It is not a legitimate general council, in which the pope[4] does not preside or another in his name." And: "All Catholics say that the function of presiding in a council belongs to the Roman pontiff, so that he himself presides over a council or through legates and guides all things as supreme judge."

Confirmation of the Thesis

We prove that the power to convoke ecumenical councils does not belong to the Roman pontiff but to the emperor or the highest political magistrate (I) by virtue of [their] office, because kings and emperors and similar people who hold high honor are divinely enjoined, Psa. 2:10-11: "Receive instruction, O ye kings. Serve Jehovah with reverence." Isa. 49:23: "Kings will be your nursing fathers and queens your nursing mothers." Cf. Deu. 17:18. Rom. 13:1: "Let every soul be subject to higher powers." 1 Ptr. 2:13: "Be ye⁵ subject to the king as ὑπερέχοντι [supreme]. Hence we argue: (1) He that convokes a council must have power over those who need to be present. But the Roman pontiff has no power over the kings and princes, who are a prominent part of the church and therefore ought to be present at the council, either personally or through legates, and their subjects. Ergo. (2) Political power belongs to the political magistrate. The power to assemble councils is a political power. Ergo. The minor [premise] is clear from this, that it presupposes power to command, summon, [and] convene, and to compel and constrain those who refuse; all these are acts of political jurisdiction. (3) He that has ecumenical power and is universal lord, his it is to assemble universal councils. Now, not the Roman pope but the emperor has ecumenical power and is universal lord. Ergo.

II. From the examples of kings and princes. In the Old Testament, assemblies and gatherings among the people of God were usually called not by Aaron the priest but by Moses the ruler of the people, and not by Eleazar but by Joshua, and therefore not by the high priests but by the judges, [and] thereafter by the kings, e.g., by David, 1 Chr. 13:1-2; 23:1-2; Solomon 1 Kin. 8:1; Hezekiah, 2 Chr. 29:4; Josiah, 2 Kin. 23:1; etc. Therefore the right to convoke councils belongs much more to Christian rulers. The conclusion is proved because the Israelite church had a high priest established by God Himself, and the right to convoke assemblies belonged to the kings. In the New Testament, Herod the king assembled a council of priests, that he might learn where the Messiah should be born. For the first three centuries after the birth of Christ the church, ἐν θλίψει [in] a state [of oppression] and lacking a Christian emperor or king, held no general councils. Yet now and then some particular ecclesiastical conventions were held, but very few, with no one convoking by jurisdiction, but solely by consensus of bishops and presbyters. But that, after that, Christian emperors convoked general councils can be proved both in general and in particular. In general from the words of Socrates [the historian], who says: "We have mentioned emperors, because from the time when they began to be Christian, affairs of the church were considered by them, and so the greatest councils" (and very many Latin editions make very much [of it]) "were convoked and still are convoked at their judgment" (τῇ αὐτῶν γνώμῃ). The same say the imperial letters and mandates and the confessions of the synods themselves, in view of the fact that they openly confess that they were assembled by authority of the emperors themselves. Jerome, when [his] adversary said that Hilary was condemned in a certain synod, said: "Say which emperor commanded this synod to assemble." By this argument he wanted to prove that the synod was not legitimately held. Specifically, the council of Nicaea was convoked by Constantine the Great, [the council of] Constantinople I by Theodosius the Elder, Ephesus I by Theodosius the Younger, Chalcedon by Emperor Marcianus, etc.

III. By the very humble supplication of the Roman pontiffs themselves. For thus writes Leo I, Roman pontiff, to Theodosius the Younger: "All the churches of our regions, all priests implore your grace with sighs and tears to command a general synod to be held in Italy," but he could not succeed, as long as Theodosius was head of the empire, in having another council besides that of Ephesus called λῃστρικὸν [robber], because of [Theodosius's] unfortunate death,[6] as Antoninus says. Leo asked the same of emperor Marcian. Gregory the Great petitioned King Theodoric in these words: "We earnestly ask again that you in turn, in accordance with your great mercy, command a synod to be assembled."

IV. From the confession of the adversaries. Cardinal Nicolaus Cusanus confesses: "Eight universal councils were convoked by emperors." Marsilius of Padua proves from the acts of the councils that this constant license and power belonged to no one but to emperors. Dominicus Jacobatius clearly says: "From the beginning the power to assemble councils belonged to the emperors." Erasmus also remarks on the words of Jerome just now cited: "Let the reader note that of old the synods usually assembled at the command of the emperors." And Bellarmine himself grants: "A general council should be convoked by him who can bring all together."

We prove that the presiding officer of a council is not necessarily the Roman bishop or his legates

I. From the example of the apostolic council, Acts 15. For there we nowhere read that Peter presided, and that alone with papal authority, but rather the director and presiding officer in the council of Jerusalem was James, who is called by the Greeks ὁ τῶν Ἱεροσολύμων ἐπίσκοπος [the bishop of Jerusalem], for he said, "I judge," Acts 15:19; he proclaims the apostolic edict. Nor does Peter speak first in the council, but when there had been much disputing, Peter arose and spoke, verse 7. And even if Peter had presided in that council, yet it is not valid to argue from Peter to the Roman pontiff.

II. From the examples of the ancient ecclesiastical councils. The *Historia Ecclesiastica* [of Eusebius] says that other bishops besides the Roman pontiff presided over most of the better known councils, especially the eight general [councils] and that the emperors themselves held the highest office, with special jurisdiction and authority. And if the emperor, tied up with other matters, was compelled to be absent, that function was in no case given to the Roman bishop but to those functionaries, τῆς εὐταξίας κατασκόποις [guardians of good order], as Constantine calls them, whom he had appointed for that office. No one is ignorant of the laudable presidency of Constantine the Great at the Council of Nicaea except he that is not at home in antiquity. And the episcopal presidents in this council were at first Eustathius of Antioch and Macarius, bishop of Jerusalem; after that, Hosius of Corduba was elected as highest ecclesiastical presiding officer and placed at the right hand of Emperor Constantine the Great, with the Roman legates Victor[7] and Vincentius falling down to his left hand. As for Hosius [as representative of the Roman pope] presiding with [the pope's] legates,[8] the conjecture is vain, there being no qualified strong witness.

In the second ecumenical council, namely Constantinople I, the presiding officer was Theodosius. But of the bishops [the following] presided, according to Photius, patriarch of Constantinople: bishops Timothy of Alexandria, Meletius of Antioch, Nectarius of Constantinople, and Cyril of Jerusalem. But the Roman pontiff did not attend this council, neither personally nor by his legates, and that Nectarius, made bishop of Constantinople in that same synod, presided, Bellarmine himself admits. Emperor Theodosius the Younger presided over the first Council of Ephesus by his legates, whom the acts of the council repeatedly call ἐξάρχους καὶ προέδρους [exarchs and presidents]. Photius says and the acts testify that of the bishops [the following] bishops presided: Cyril of Alexandria, Memnon of Ephesus, and Juvenal of Jerusalem. Bellarmine holds that Celestine, Roman pontiff, presided by his legate Cyril. But Cyril presided over the whole synod by general and extraordinary presidency according to the wish of the council. He outranked also his patriarch Celestine by the extraordinary assignment of Celestine himself by fraternal office.[9] And though the Synod of Ephesus often mentions Celestine, yet it nowhere honors him with the title of president, in fact it clearly calls him συνεδρεύοντα, the assistant, not πρόεδρεύοντα, president. Besides the acts of the council, Evagrius says that emperor Marcian conducted[10] the [external course of the proceedings of the] fourth general council, which is that of Chalcedon, through consular men, which he himself had set up as judges. As to faith, or internal matters, the following guided it [the council]: bishops Anatolius of Constantinople, Maximus of Antioch, and Juvenal of Jerusalem. First Anatolius, in second place the vicars of Leo announced decisions. Briefly, a general ecclesiastical president was clearly not elected at the Council of Chalcedon but individual patriarchs outranked the bishops of their patriarchate. One finds no, or at any rate slight, indications in any [writers] that the Roman popes held the presidency in later ecumenical councils assembled by the emperors. (For we disregard anti-Christian councils.)

III. From the circumstances of the Roman pontiff. For monarchic power over all bishops does not belong by divine right to the Roman pontiff. Therefore it is not absolutely necessary that he be president of all councils. At the time of the [papal] schism there was no authoritative pope. Therefore in that case a Roman pontiff could not preside in the councils. For a doubtful pope is regarded as a nonpope. Pierre Du Moulin says: "The Roman pontiff never attended the ancient universal councils, but sent legates, who were called τοπτηρέτας [literally: wardens of a place], who presided with his legates. They sat in the common assembly and did not preside over the councils. The reasons why the Roman bishops did not want to attend the universal councils were these: namely because in these councils all matters were handled in the Greek language, of which language the Roman bishops were ignorant. But mainly so that it would not be for them to fight about προεδρία [precedence] with the bishop of Constantinople, who called himself universal bishop and competed with the rank of the Roman bishop."

Vindication

Bellarmine objects (I): "Princes are prominent only in matters that make for the political state, and Christian princes do not preside over Christians insofar as they are Christians but insofar as they are human beings. For princes themselves, insofar as they are Christians, are sheep and therefore subject to shepherds." We reply: (1) God Himself teaches, Psa. 2:10; Deu. 17:19; Isa. 49:23, that a king is prominent also in those matters that concern the house of God, so that it might be properly managed. (2) It is false that Christian kings do not rule Christians insofar as they are Christians but insofar as they are human beings, since Paul commands that prayers be poured out for the kings and for all who are set in high places, that we might live a peaceful life under them ἐν πασῃ εὐσεβείᾳ [in all godliness], 1 Tim. 2:1–2. (3) In actions that serve the ecclesiastical government inwardly, such as are the preaching of the Word, the administration of the sacraments, the administration of the loosing and binding key, the king is not the father, but a son, not a shepherd, but a sheep, not a lord but a subject, according to the example of David, 2 Sam. 12:1ff. But where matters concern the outward government of the church, the ruling power certainly belongs to the emperors, kings, and princes. (II) Bellarmine objects: "The kings of Israel and Judah, by extraordinary authority, had right and power not only in political but also in ecclesiastical matters, and they used it not only as kings but also as prophets." We reply: Nonsense. For Hezekiah was not a prophet but a king. And extraordinary authority cannot be expanded. For in Deu. 17:19 the king is enjoined so to rule his subjects that his obligation toward God would be properly met, as is clear from the example of Hezekiah, 2 Kin. 18:6. (III) Bellarmine objects: "Those first four ecumenical councils were indeed convoked by the emperors, but that was done according to the wish and with the consent of the Roman pontiff." We reply: We have said above that the question is not about the consent of the ecclesiastical ministry in convoking synods but about the jurisdiction and authority of bringing councils together. Consent is not authority. Other bishops also consented, and yet they did not have the highest power. Thus Rufinus writes: "Constantine convoked the council according to the wish of the priests." And that was not of necessity but of free will and imperial grace toward the Roman bishop, if his consent was requested, since sometimes also without consent, or with the Roman bishop rather asking and begging something else, the emperor moved to action in convoking synods, as the example of Leo I shows. Others retort: "The emperors were executors of the apostolic see, not the authors of such a matter." But this cannot be said without violence to the truth of history. (IV) They object "(1) Constantine the Great signed after all the bishops. Therefore he was not president. (2) He did not dare to sit except in a seat lower than were [those] of the bishops, in fact he sat below the bishops (according to Binius) and with their assent." We reply: They are mere conjectures, the first of which is doubly inept: (1) In mixing disparates.[11] A president of action is one thing, one of order [is] another. Hosius, bishop of Corduba, signed first, but Constantine [as the] last wanted to ratify the acts by his signature. (2) In setting nonopposites in opposition.¹² Those things do not conflict in any way: Constantine signed after all the bishops; therefore he did not preside. For sometimes also the president, having obtained the signature of individuals, was wont to sign last for a very good reason. The second [objection] assumes something [but] proves nothing. For who will convince us that the seat of Constantine was lower than [those] of the bishops? And Theodoret and Eusebius, both praised by Bellarmine and Baronius, speak of μίκρῳ θρόνῳ [a little throne], which Constantine had occupied to avoid displaying imperial pride in that assembly, so that he might be present as one of the assembly. But granted that he sat lowest, does a lower seat therefore take anything away from the imperial rank? For, as Baronius himself admits: "The inferior place was the most honorable of all among the ancients." Moreover, "he did not dare to sit except when the bishops assented" is said without basis. The words of Eusebius, οὐ πρώτερον ἢ τοὺς ἐπισκόπους ἐπινεῖσαι ἐκάθισε [he did not sit before the bishops nodded assent], do not imply permission obtained from the emperor to sit, but as a sign from those who expected to sit down together, lest, with him seated, the bishops would stand, who would sit down later. Eusebius says: "ταυτὸν δ᾽ἔπραττον πάντες μετὰ τὸν βασιλέα, all did the same after the emperor." Theodoret says: "σὺν αὐτῷ [with him], the bishops sat down together and at the same time."

Refutation of Objections

I. Bellarmine objects: "A council is not legitimate unless it is assembled in the name of Christ, Mat. 18:20. And to be assembled in the name of Christ is to be assembled by the authority of Christ by him who has from Christ the authority to assemble, because 'in the name' is the same as 'by the authority.' Now, Christ entrusted the church not to Tiberius but to Peter and his successors, John 21:17: 'Feed My sheep.'" We reply: (1) In Mat. 18:20 Christ neither speaks of public synods, since two or three are by no means enough to constitute them, nor does He point out any head or say whose it is to assemble synods; He says only who and what kind of assemblies, however small, might look for an assured answer, namely those who gather in the name of Christ. (2) To gather in the name of Christ does not mean only by the command and authority of Christ, but [it means] especially to gather in the faith and invocation of Christ; this is clear (1) from the added promise of [His] gracious presence; (2) from the connection with the preceding verse and the αἰτιολογία [assignment of a cause or reason] in [the verse] that follows [the preceding verse]: "For where," etc. (3) If to convoke in the name of Christ is the same as by authority of the pope, then it would follow that the first four universal councils were not convoked in the name of Christ, because they were convoked not by the pope but by the emperors. (4) It is completely false that the care of the whole church was entrusted only to Peter and his fictitious successor, the Roman pontiff. (5) We have pointed out above that the passage in John 21:17, "Feed My sheep," is cited ἀπροσδιονύσως [beside the point] and the right to feed does not mean any dominion but rather ministry, which consists in preaching.

II. They object: "It is his to assemble general councils who can bring all together, because no emperor ever had the whole church subject to himself, also with regard to civil actions as the [Roman] pontiff has it with regard to spiritual actions." We reply: (1) No pontiff ever had the whole church subject [to himself]. (2) The hypothesis of the argument consists in the primacy of the pope, which has not yet been proved. (3) What is asserted regarding the compulsory and universal power of the Roman pontiff is false, as is clear from examples and decrees of the councils. (4) No one could bring together a universal council before there was a Christian emperor. (5) When we ascribe to the emperor supreme and preeminent power in this matter, we do not exclude the voices of lesser powers. (6) The pope could not even convoke the Gallican bishops in the conciliabulum of Trent without the permission of the king of Gaul. (7) Nowhere in the accounts does one read that any bishops were called together into a council except the Western [bishops] in the Roman patriarchate.

III. They object: The provincial councils were convoked by a metropolitan and national [councils] by a primate or patriarch; therefore general councils are to be convoked not by the emperor but by the highest pontiff. Thus Bellarmine. We reply: (1) Bringing together councils, both particular and universal, belongs principally to the magistrate, who nevertheless ought not scorn the counsel and views of theologians in this matter. But if the magistrate defers and commits his rights to bishops, the bishops can indeed use that right, however not as lords but as servants of a superior power. If, therefore, primates or archbishops [and] bishops convoked councils, they did that not by their own authority but delegated [authority] or that which they arrogated to themselves, *de facto* [in fact], not *de jure* [by right]. (2) According to the ancient canons, the Roman pontiff is only bishop of the first see, not a monarch but a patriarch. He can therefore convoke nothing else than a national council.

IV. Binius, Bellarmine, and other pontiffs try to prove that Sylvester assembled [the Council of] Nicaea by his command and Damasus the Council of Constantinople, because in the sixth general synod, or Constantinople III, it is said that Constantine and Sylvester συνέλεγον, assembled the Synod of Nicaea and that Emperor Theodosius and Damasus, Gregory, and Nectarius convoked Constantinople I. We reply: (1) Binius himself confesses that the proceedings of this council are corrupt in many places. Albert Pighius shows in a special treatise that these proceedings are interpolated or surreptitious. (3) Melchior Canus is painstaking in disproving the authority of this council. (4) Nothing else shows up out of the words of this council, if they are true, than that the Roman bishops did in their districts toward gathering these synods what Gregory of Nazianzus and Nectarius of Constantinople did, since by one and the same term these are said to have assembled the council; therefore no preeminence is there ascribed to the pontiff.

V. They object: "All the bishops in the fourth Council of Rome, convoked by King Theodoric, claimed that the synod should have been convoked not by the king but by the pope, even if the pope be under accusation." We reply: (1) In this council Pope Symmachus was both defendant and judge, [and] the bishops were sycophants of the pope. One can therefore easily see how much is to be assigned to this synod. (2) Nevertheless it was necessary for the bishops to gather in the synod in response to the command of the king; by this the power of the political magistrate in this question is confirmed.

VI. Bellarmine also adduces some testimonies of pontiffs and the reply of Emperor Valentinian, who, [when] asked by the bishops where he would allow them to hold a council, said: "It is not my province to investigate such matters in greater detail. Priests, convene wherever you want to." We reply: (1) Pontiffs are not qualified witnesses in their own cause. (2) Inasmuch as the bishops request of Emperor Valentinian the power to hold a council, by that very fact they show that this function belongs to the emperor. (3) As to Valentinian refusing to accept for himself the responsibility of religion, we cannot prove that he did this as a favor to his Arian brother Valens.

VII. Bellarmine objects: "The highest pontiff is the shepherd and father of the whole church to the point that also all bishops and princes are called sheep and sons with regard to the highest pontiff. Now, fathers ought to preside over sons and shepherds over sheep." We reply: (1) The Roman pontiff neither feeds sheep nor begets spiritual children by the preaching of the Word. Therefore he is neither a shepherd nor a father but rather a wolf and a wicked stepfather. (2) Christ alone is the shepherd and father of the universal church, John 10:11, 14; Mat. 23:8–9. (3) To feed the sheep of Christ does not mean universal rule of the church or supreme presidency over councils, otherwise there would be as many lords and presidents as there are shepherds. (4) In some councils the bishops indeed called the pope father, but not of the whole church. And (5) this title was attached also to other patriarchs. This goes in a circle. The pope should preside because he is the highest pontiff and the shepherd and head of all. And the pope is the pontiff, shepherd, and head of all because he presides over councils. Both are arguments of Bellarmine. The emperor and the princes are not only sheep but also nursing fathers of the church and thus also of the shepherds.

Therefore kings and princes assemble shepherds by the same right as that by which they nourish, not by feeding the church but by seeing that they are properly fed.

VIII. They object: "Peter presided in the apostolic council, Acts 15. Therefore his successor, the Roman pontiff, has the right to preside in councils." We reply: (1) We have shown the contrary above in the Confirmation [of the theses], num. I. (2) Before Peter arose there was a great argument, v. 7. (3) Jerome calls Peter the author of the apostolic decree because, after he had related the account that is in Acts 10, the hearts of very many were moved. (4) It is not valid [to argue] from Peter to the Roman pontiff.

IX. They object: The Roman pontiff presided in the ecumenical councils. We reply: We have showed the contrary in the Confirmation [of the theses], num. II.

Notes:

[1] "An ecclesiastical council assembled without or against the authority of the legitimate ecclesiastical superior;—disting. from council" (Webst. 2d unabr.).
[2] *Pontifex maximus.*
[3] *qui eius locum tenent.*
[4] *Pontifex.*
[5] To indicate the plural.
[6] He died July 28, 450, after a fall from his horse.
[7] Latin text: *Vito.* Cf. Hefele, *Conciliengeschichte,* 2d ed., I, p. 292, line 11.
[8] Cf. Herzog-Hauck, *Realencyklopädie,* 3d ed., VIII, p. 378, lines 33–34.
[9] *ex officio fraterno.*
[10] *rexit.*
[11] *non mixta miscendo.*
[12] *Non opposita opponendo.*

www.ingramcontent.com/pod-product-compliance
Lightning Source LLC
LaVergne TN
LVHW020931090426
835512LV00020B/3314